About the authors

JOHN SYMONDS is a keen fly-fisherman and fishes for salmon, trout and grayling in the Wye and Usk catchments as well as the Welsh borderlands. He decided to become a certified casting instructor and guide as a retirement occupation and has successfully qualified to Advanced Professional Game Angling Instructors (APGAI) single- and double-handed levels, and is an International Federation of Fly Fishers (FFF) Two-Handed Casting Instructor (THCI). Philip Maher was John's mentor throughout the period leading up to achieving these qualifications and it is hoped that this book will be a useful manual for those following the same path. Using his graphic and photographic skills, John has been able to convey on paper – in a clear, accessible style – the current methods used for teaching students how to cast.

PHILIP MAHER grew up by the River Suir at Ballycamus, Ireland, where he mastered the art of dry fly fishing for wild brown trout on slow-moving water, where presentation and accuracy are essential. Philip's skills were apparent from an early age. He won the first of many Munster Juvenile River Championships at the age of 8, going on to win All-Ireland Senior in 1995 at the age of 20. He was Captain of the Irish Team in the 1996 World Championships in the Czech Republic, finishing top Irish rod.

Already a proficient angler, Philip sought to understand more fully the mechanics and techniques of casting. He took the Federation of Fly Fishers (FFF) exams, passing both his Certified and Masters Fly Casting Instructor qualifications in one weekend. Subsequently he passed both his salmon and trout Advanced Professional Game Angling Instructors (APGAI) exams.

Philip runs his own tackle and flyfishing tuition business – FishHunt – near Clonmel, Tipperary.

FLYCASTING
SKILLS

for beginner and expert

John Symonds & Philip Maher

MERLIN UNWIN BOOKS

First published by Merlin Unwin Books, 2013

Text © John Symonds and Philip Maher 2013
Illustrations © John Symonds 2013

Merlin Unwin Books Limited
Palmers' House, 7 Corve Street,
Ludlow, Shropshire, SY8 1DB

www.merlinunwin.co.uk

A CIP record of this book is available from the British Library.

Designed by John Symonds
www.fly-fish-guide.net

Printed and bound by 1010 Printing International Ltd

ISBN 9781906122492

Contents

Contents *continued*

Foreword

Flycasting Skills could not have been written without the exceptional expertise, wisdom and combined experience of co-authors, John Symonds and Philip Maher.

Philip combines the experience of a lifetime of fly-fishing and fly-casting tuition with impressive advanced certifications. He is a Federation of Fly Fishers Master Casting Instructor who has also been certified as a Two-Handed Casting Instructor by the same organization. The Association of Professional Game Angling Instructors has certified him in Single- and Two-Handed casting instruction as well as Fly Dressing.

This text had its infancy in the notes taken by John Symonds as the two authors worked together on the water while casting, fishing and critically discussing the details of each cast.

John's credentials are impressive. He has achieved APGAI double- and single-handed casting certification and FFF two-handed casting instructor certification. Along with his advanced knowledge of fly-casting and technical expertise, John has produced the wonderfully clear graphics, which enrich the text and assist in making the casts so easy for both student and instructor to understand. These depictions reflect the long hours spent with Philip as they worked together on the river.

In addition to expert fly-casting instruction, the authors provide invaluable information on a wide range of related topics such as fly rod and fly line characteristics, casting terms, casting mechanics and line management.

Flycasting Skills will complement the authors' on the water fly-casting instruction. It is a significant publication, which will serve as a reference for fly-casters, students of fly-casting and instructors everywhere.

Gordy Hill
Florida, USA

Federation of Fly Fishers Master Certified Instructor
and member of the FFF Board of Governors

How to use this book

Flycasting Skills teaches all levels of fisher — from complete beginner, to expert, and even casting instructor — how to master a wide range of different casts to match all conditions and challenges.

Some prefer to learn 'visually', and this book has been designed to teach by simply looking at the clear graphic images and digesting the instruction in that way.

For those who like the additional reassurance of a written explanation, the moves are also described fully, usually on the facing page. There is also a variety of useful tips and advice given here in the fact panels.

And for those who like to understand why the rod and line react together in the way that they do, when manipulated by the caster, then there is a brief section of further reading at the back of this book which, in simple terms, outlines the physics of casting, the basic lesson in loading energy in the fly-line via the rod. It is not essential to know how a cast works, but it can help some people to cast better — it all depends on the individual.

So enjoy picking and mixing through this book, learning in the way that works for you.

John Symonds

Symbols used in diagrams

	Direction of water flow
	Wind direction
	Body line – an imaginary line between caster and target Casting line – direction of forward cast Lift line – imaginary line for initial lift of fly-line
	The fly rod, shown in its straight position i.e. unflexed and with orange circles which indicate top and bottom hand positions
	The river with a red spot which is used to indicate the imaginary anchor position of the line-tip
	Fly-line
	Anchor placement movement – used to indicate how the rod-tip is moved, with slow acceleration, from the lift position to the waterborne anchor position
	Setting up movement – used to indicate how the rod-tip is swept, with medium/fast acceleration, from the lift position or the waterborne anchor position to the D-loop position
	Forward cast movement – the final horizontal stroke with fast acceleration used to form the forward loop

Introduction

Flyfishing is an absorbing sport, steeped in tradition, with an inexhaustible amount of available knowledge for those that want it. Game anglers get a great deal of satisfaction from constructing the 'perfect' fly, or buying the best tackle, or simply being by or in the water. It is an idyllic sport and it doesn't even really matter if it is done badly, providing the angler's dream is fulfilled.

However, those who know about flyfishing will tell you that, once you have established where the fish are, the main requirement for success is to fish the fly at the correct depth and at the correct speed. OK, the colour and size of your fly might indeed increase the odds of catching but, in my view, far too much emphasis is given to those factors – simply because they are easy to comprehend, visualise and apply. How often do we *really* know how deep we are fishing?

Anglers shy away from learning to cast properly because it is more difficult to understand and it cannot be learnt sitting by the fireside, drinking a glass of malt. Many hours of practice, standing in the river, are required to reach an acceptable level of casting competence. Furthermore, casting is not an easy subject to learn from a book because the concepts are difficult to explain in words.

So, how *do* you learn to present the fly correctly, in the right spot, with a drag-free drift and at the right depth? By learning to cast effectively, of course!

This book began as a series of notes, which I wrote to remind myself of the essential information required to understand how the fly-rod and line work together and how to improve my casting. At first the ideas were a collection of facts, some of which were self-evident, and others that I didn't fully understand but they seemed to produce good results. Then I met up with Philip Maher who is a Fly Fishing Federation (FFF) Master and an Advanced Professional Game Angling Instructor (APGAI) and he was able to provide plenty of practical experience as a teacher of single- and double-handed casting.

After many enjoyable trips to Ireland and numerous photo sessions on the rivers Suir and Blackwater, with Philip's knowledge and my graphic skills, we were able to compile this book. It aims to provide the flyfisher with essential information and tips that will lead to better casting. Some of the information is also suitable for instructors.

Unlike all other flycasting books before it, our book shows all the main casts – step-by-step, on a single page, with explanatory notes. This is as close as it gets (in book form) to instruction in real life and it is supported by the theory that will help you fully understand *why* the cast works. The book is therefore an ideal accompaniment to a casting lesson given by an instructor.

Here then are the essential casting skills required by the flyfisher, to complement those other useful skills such as entomology, flytying, weather-forecasting and the ability to tell tall tales!

John Symonds
November 2012

Holding the single-handed fly rod

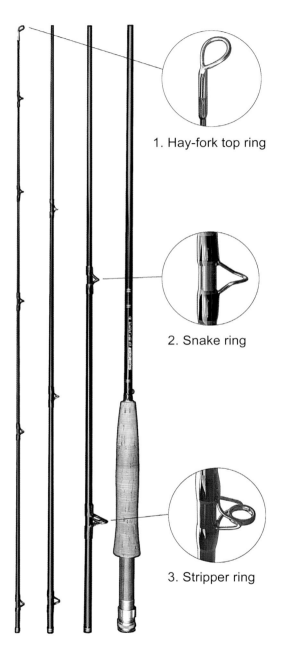

1. Hay-fork top ring

2. Snake ring

3. Stripper ring

Above: A typical four section fly-rod, 9ft #6 rating suitable for general-purpose trout fishing.

Comfort is the most important consideration when the fly rod is used for several hours. It must be held in a relaxed manner whilst at rest and in action.

Casting comprises two basic movements: a horizontal stroke at the beginning of the cast, followed by a rotation of the rod handle, around an imaginary pivot point. Therefore your hand position must accommodate these two movements.

Gripping single-handed rods

A number of grip styles can be used with a single-handed rod. One of the most common is the **thumb on top grip**. Pressure is applied through the thumb to create powerful rod rotation. The drawback with this grip is that in the open stance casting position (which is used for longer casting) the hand is naturally turned if the thumb is on top, and this causes the wrist to twist during the forward cast.

Thumb on top grip

Another method employs the **index finger on top**, which helps to prevent wrist break. Some anglers find it helps them to cast accurately.

This grip makes it more difficult to cast a long line, due to the relative weakness of the index finger.

Index finger on top grip

The **Three point contact** is one of the most efficient and popular grips. It allows unimpaired movement when casting.

The rod is held loosely in the hand and simply allowed to snap forward under its own weight during rod rotation.

The three point contact grip provides better overall control with less chance of wrist rotation.

Any of the grips mentioned may be used if they are comfortable and fulfil the requirements of the casting style.

Whatever grip is selected, it should be relaxed and comfortable, providing control of the wrist, and thus good loop formation. The grip should be loose (like holding a small bird), except at the end of the stroke when a crisper stop can be achieved by squeezing the hand, followed by releasing the grip again to dampen out any rod-tip vibration.

In all three examples listed, the wrist is shown in the locked position with the rod butt almost touching the underside of the forearm. The wrist is cocked ever so slightly at the beginning of the forward cast and the end of the back cast, thus providing essential, linear, wrist rotation. Under no circumstances should the wrist be allowed to flop because this will dissipate the energy that is stored in the fly-rod.

Three point contact grip

Casting terms

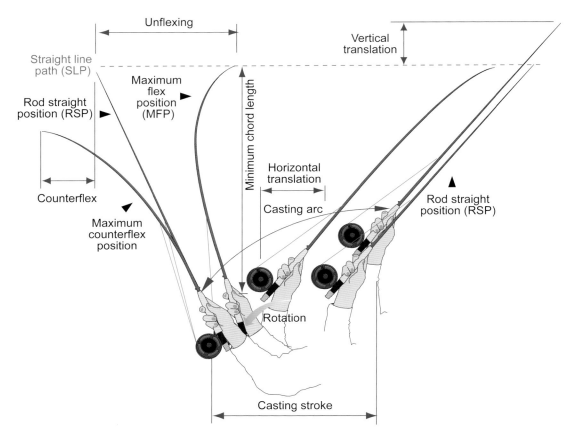

The main terms used to describe a cast

When casting, to create a tight loop, the two main objectives are to maintain a *straight line path (SLP)* and to continuously accelerate the rod-tip to a stop. The straight line path ensures that force is always applied in the direction of the cast. Acceleration ensures that the fly-line is always under control and that the fly rod is loaded.

The *rod straight position (RSP)* is when the fly rod is not being flexed. This occurs at the beginning and the end of the casting cycle.

The *maximum flex position (MFP)* will occur when there is a *minimum chord length*, which is the distance between the rod-handle and the rod-tip. This represents the minimum effective

rod length and so should be at vertical to give the maximum height above the ground (or water) so that the *straight line path (SLP)* is maintained. It is at this position that the stop is normally applied.

Casting stroke describes the distance that the rod hand travels from the beginning to the end of the cast and this is a useful measure because it has to be adjusted depending upon the length of fly-line outside the rod-tip and distance of the cast. To aerialise more fly-line requires a longer *casting stroke*.

Translation is the term used to describe the forward movement of the fly rod when it is not rotating in the direction of the casting line.

Effectively, every point on the rod moves the same distance in the same direction. Most of the time translation and linear rotation occur simultaneously but there is one distinct translation which is used at the beginning of the cast and in the diagram this is referred to as *vertical translation*. This is a vertical movement of the rod, achieved by dropping the elbow in the case of a single-handed fly rod or both hands for a double-handed fly rod before stroking forward and rotation. The action drops the rod-tip to the straight line path from its final, high position at the end of the back-cast. It also allows the fly-line to fall under the effect of gravity so that it aligns with the straight line path.

Horizontal translation takes place as the casting hand (or top hand on a double-handed fly rod) moves forward for a distance that is determined by the casting stroke and length of fly-line aerialised.

Rotation of the fly rod in the direction of the cast makes the major contribution to rod-tip speed. It also maintains the *straight line path (SLP)* of the rod-tip as the fly rod flexes during loading and unflexes at the end of the cast. The amount of *rotation* is indicated by the *casting arc*. It is the angle that the rod butt rotates through the cast.

The fly rod is *constantly accelerated* to create progressive *rod loading* until it reaches the *maximum flex position (MFP)* where further travel is stopped abruptly, allowing the fly rod to *unflex*. Even though there is a stop, because of the dynamics, the fly rod will continue to travel, but it will decelerate and this allows the energy to be transferred to the fly-line, which occurs at peak velocity, a point somewhere between *maximum flex position (MFP)* and the *rod straight position (RSP)*. Following this the fly rod goes into *counterflex* and the distance of the rod-tip below the *straight line path* at the *maximum counterflex position* determines the shape of the fly-line loop. In most instances a compact loop is desired so it is important to keep the rod-tip as high as possible at the rod straight position after *counterflex*, which can be helped by lifting the fly rod in the direction of the cast.

The stop is used to extend the *casting stroke* length to its maximum, whilst maintaining a *straight line path (SLP)* which is essential for a narrow loop. After the stop the fly rod will unflex at a speed which is determined by its recovery time.

Useful casting rules

The following rules must be followed in order to cast with a good loop:

- The rod-tip must follow a straight line path from the beginning to the end of the stroke.

- There must be no slack in the fly-line.

- A sufficient pause must be allowed at the end of each casting stroke to allow the fly-line to unroll (or for a D-loop to form).

- The correct length of casting stroke and arc must be used for the length of fly-line outside the rod-tip.

- The fly rod must be accelerated to an abrupt stop to generate sufficient energy and to transfer this to the aerialised fly-line.

For Spey casts:

The **180° rule** must be applied. It states that:

- Your feet should face in the general direction of the target.

- The D-loop must be aligned with the forward casting line.

- The anchor must also be aligned with the casting line.

For Spey casts the anchor should be:

- The minimum amount required to provide sufficient line stick to hold the D-loop and this may be just the leader.

- A distance of 1 to 1½ rod's length off the casting shoulder and just in front of the caster.

The Key Position (single-handed fly rod)

The two pictures on this page show the key positions for a single-handed rod. **All conventional forward casts start like this**, with the elbow raised slightly and closed, the forearm up vertical and the wrist slightly cocked. The casting hand is positioned so that it can be seen out of the corner of the eye and by looking at the rod-butt it is easy to check the inclination of the fly rod.

When casting, the objective is to manipulate the fly rod so that it ends up in the right (the key) position for making the final delivery of the fly-line towards the target.

From this position the rod tip can be easily accelerated forward, along a straight line path: both of which are essential requirements for loading the fly rod and forming a tight forward loop. The casting elbow should be tucked in close to the side of the body, to give precise control and maximum use of energy.

If the wind is blowing from the casting arm side, then it is possible to make all casts by moving

the key position over to the other side of the body *(above right)*. To achieve this the elbow has to be raised slightly higher, otherwise the same hand position is adopted, on the other side of the body, and the forward cast is made in the same manner as the normal cast.

Alternatively, the casting hand can remain on the normal side and the fly rod can be canted over so that the fly-line rests on the other side of the body. This is a question of personal preference.

It is important to practice setting up the **key position**, using a static roll cast for instance, because it has to occur automatically at the end of most casting sequences – as will be seen in the numerous examples illustrated in this book.

The Key Position (double-handed fly rod)

The two pictures on this page show the **key position** with the right-hand uppermost or with the left-hand uppermost. A two-handed caster must be proficent with either hand uppermost because he has no control over the wind direction or the side of the river that he is given to fish.

A conventional forward cast always starts from the key position and so all other rod movements up to this moment in a casting sequence are used for setting up the fly rod and fly-line so that the caster ends up holding the two-handed fly rod as shown in the picture, ready to make the final delivery of the fly-line towards the target.

The top hand is positioned so that it can be just seen out of the corner of the eye (to help beginners remember this position: it can be described as like answering the telephone), with the top forearm almost vertical and the top hand holding the fly rod lightly. The bottom hand is pushed forward in front of the centre-line of the body, with the forearm almost horizontal but should not cross over to the other half of the body. This should also grip the fly rod softly.

Without looking at the fly rod it is possible to check its inclination by looking at the angle of the butt.

As a guide, for a static roll cast, the fly rod can be inclined at 45°, depending upon rod action and the length of fly-line being cast.

The feet should face in the general direction of the forward cast, although in a strong flow of water some variation may be necessary, to give balance and stability. Hand spacing can be determined by holding the fly rod in the rest position with the arms hanging down the sides of the body in a relaxed position, resting the fly rod in the palms of the hands.

During the cast, the top hand will act as a fulcrum and the bottom hand will be used to induce a fast rod-tip velocity, which will create fly rod loading and cause it to flex.

Casting tip

A competent caster should be capable of casting with either the right or the left hand uppermost and should practice until this becomes second nature.

Acceleration to a stop (single-handed fly rod)

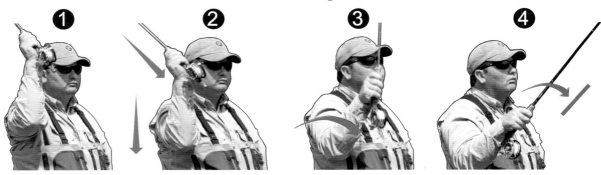

Continuous acceleration of the rod tip is required for loading the fly rod. This must be followed by an abrupt stop to ensure that the energy in the loaded fly rod is transferred as quickly as possible to the fly-line. The quicker the transfer of energy, the tighter the resulting forward loop.

To visualise and apply continuous acceleration to a rod tip is difficult. It is achieved by stepping up the velocity by a series of hand and arm movements. The **key position** is so important here because it places the arm and hand(s) where they are ready to do this efficiently and automatically, without the caster having to think about it.

Starting from the key position, with a single-handed fly rod, the first move involves dropping the elbow and moving the hand forward. Initially the casting hand and fly rod maintain, more or less, the same inclination, with the wrist in the slightly cocked position, causing the rod tip to move with the same instantaneous velocity as the hand (which is relatively slow). Instructors may sometimes refer to this as **translation**.

The instantaneous velocity can now be increased by pivoting the forearm at the elbow in the direction of the cast, with the wrist still cocked, and this causes the rod tip to begin to rotate, and move quicker.

Finally the rod tip velocity is brought up to a maximum by pivoting the wrist in the direction of the cast. Leverage is achieved by using the thumb side of the hand to represent the "top hand" and the fifth (or little) finger to represent the "lower hand" used in two-handed casting.

By merging all of these movements into one smooth sequence, acceleration is achieved. It is important to understand that the fastest rod tip speed is achieved in the burst of energy leading up to the **stop**, and up until this point the casting action is relatively slow. The moment of maximum momentum of the fly rod is very short. Many unskilled casters do not appreciate this fact and so they put far too much momentum into the whole cast.

The stop is applied when the imaginary chord between the rod tip and the rod-butt *(see Casting terms page 4)* is at a minimum. A close approximation to the action of the **stop** is that of flicking something off the rod tip. If you grip the fly rod butt hard at the moment the stop is applied and then relax it immediately afterwards this will reduce the tendency of waves to form in the fly-line as it is cast out.

Another essential requirement of a good cast is to keep a straight line path of rod tip from the **key position** to the **stop** and after. The rod tip should be stopped high and then dropped to follow the fly-line down as it rolls out. Stopping high will reduce the effects of fly rod shake and ripples in the fly-line.

Acceleration to a stop (double-handed fly rod)

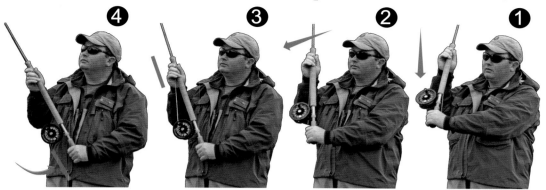

The series of pictures above show the hand and arm movements that are used to accelerate the rod tip of a double-handed fly rod. They show the caster in the key position with the right hand up **[1]**. Prior to this his hands would have been held higher as a result of setting up the D-loop, and so the first move involves dropping the hands, vertically, to the key position.

Next the top hand is moved forward a short distance **[2]** causing the rod tip to move slowly and then it comes to a distinct stop. The bottom hand then takes over **[3]**, pulling in towards the body, and the fly rod pivots around the top hand causing the rod tip to speed up due to the rotary motion of the fly rod. Towards the end of this movement the bottom hand is pulled back rapidly **[4]** and then stopped, blocking further movement of the rod butt and causing the fly rod to unload rapidly, transferring energy to the fly-line.

Throughout the forward cast the rod tip should trace a straight line path and it can be seen in the example that the fly rod is stopped when the rod tip is still high, for this reason. The sequence is continuous and should start off slowly with very rapid acceleration at the end of the cast before the abrupt stop, to create a tight loop.

Common mistakes

Beginners are inclined to use more of the top-hand to make a cast but this has a number of limitations. Firstly, it is more difficult to maintain a straight line path of the rod tip. Secondly, it is more difficult to apply an abrupt stop with the hand pushing away, rather than pulling in towards the body. Thirdly, it makes it more difficult to introduce the rotary motion that is essential for inducing a high rod tip speed.

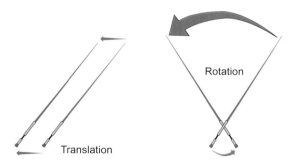

The diagram above shows how the rod tip speed can be increased dramatically by switching from a linear rod movement (translation) to a rotary movement (rotation). These two movements are combined in the forward cast to create maximum rod loading (flex), a high rod tip velocity (kinetic energy), which is then transferred to the fly-line by the stop.

Single-handed lift

This cast is frequently used in stillwater fly-fishing – a simple pick-up and lay-down to represent the fly.

Start with the rod tip close to the water's surface [1]. If there is no slack in the fly-line, the maximum amount of rod loading is achieved. As the rod tip is lifted [2] there will be some resistance caused by the surface tension of the water, which will cause the fly rod to load, and as soon as the water tension can hold the fly rod no longer it will be at the point of maximum loading and so the stop should be applied immediately [3]. By stopping the fly rod at this position, the fly-line will continue to travel in a straight-line path but one that is sloping steeply upwards and backwards [4]. It is also necessary to accelerate the rod tip faster than normal, up to the stop, to achieve the desired rod-loading.

As the fly-line travels back, the casting hand should be allowed to drift upwards, ensuring that the line straightens out and has sufficient height to allow it to drop before making the forward cast [5]. The latter will be along a straight-line path with a more level trajectory depending on the length of cast and the strength and direction of the prevailing wind.

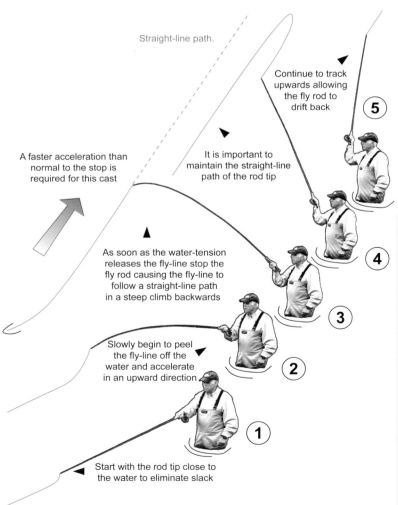

Straight-line path.

Continue to track upwards allowing the fly rod to drift back

A faster acceleration than normal to the stop is required for this cast

It is important to maintain the straight-line path of the rod tip

As soon as the water-tension releases the fly-line stop the fly rod causing the fly-line to follow a straight-line path in a steep climb backwards

Slowly begin to peel the fly-line off the water and accelerate in an upward direction

Start with the rod tip close to the water to eliminate slack

To change direction

A change of direction (up to 30°) can be made with this cast by facing in the direction of the new cast, placing the rod tip close to the water's surface and pointing it in the direction of the final target. The fly rod is then lifted in the conventional manner, even though the fly-line is at an angle to the new casting-line. A longer pause is required to allow the fly-line to straighten before making the forward cast.

Double-handed lift

Start in a relaxed position with the arms hanging down and the fly rod resting in the hands. The rod tip should be close to the water's surface ► **1**

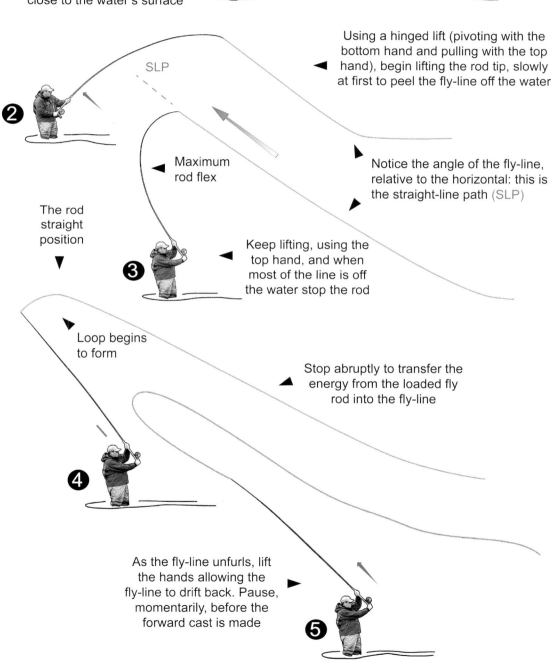

Using a hinged lift (pivoting with the bottom hand and pulling with the top hand), begin lifting the rod tip, slowly at first to peel the fly-line off the water ◄

SLP

2

Maximum rod flex ◄

Notice the angle of the fly-line, relative to the horizontal: this is the straight-line path (SLP) ►

The rod straight position ▼

3 Keep lifting, using the top hand, and when most of the line is off the water stop the rod ◄

► Loop begins to form

Stop abruptly to transfer the energy from the loaded fly rod into the fly-line ◄

4

As the fly-line unfurls, lift the hands allowing the fly-line to drift back. Pause, momentarily, before the forward cast is made ►

5

Pause and drift

Whilst the fly-line is rolling out, after the fly rod has been stopped, a pause is required before starting the next cast in the opposite direction. This is necessary for the efficient loading of the fly rod. Coming back too early will either cause the fly-line to collapse or to 'crack' because of the whiplash effect.

This pause can be used to great effect for extending the amount of rod-tip travel during the subsequent cast, which means that it is possible to cast a longer fly-line and it cushions the initial loading on the fly rod, resulting in a smoother casting action. This is achieved by following the fly-line upwards with the rod tip. It is referred to as 'drifting'.

Single-handed

The elbow is raised to allow the fly-line to 'drift' back, giving it time to unfurl in readiness for the forward cast. It also increases stroke length on the forward cast. ▶

Double-handed

Both hands are raised, backwards, to allow the fly-line to 'drift' back, giving it time to unfurl in readiness for the forward cast. This also increases stroke length on the forward cast. ▶

The diagrams above show how the hands and fly rod move in the same direction as the fly-line to create 'drift'. Single-handed and double-handed fly rods are both shown.

Overhead cast

Casting backwards and forwards, over the head, is one of the first methods of casting that will be attempted by the beginner because it gets the fly out onto the water.

Overhead casting is very suitable for stillwater fishing, but it is limited in terms of changing direction. Furthermore, a reasonable amount of space is required behind the caster for the back cast. However, the simple overhead cast does have a lot of practical value when it comes to learning about fly casting.

The false cast

False casting (continuous forward and backward casting) helps the caster to understand the principles of timing, casting stroke, casting arc, the pause, power application and the straight-line path.

An excellent way of practicing false casting is to start with a closed stance, a very short length of fly-line outside the rod-tip and to adjust the stroke so that the fly-line just rolls out both ways with symmetrical, narrow loops. Not as easy as it sounds because there is a natural tendency to use too much effort and to move the rod-tip further than necessary. Initially, your loops will be too wide and so the amount of rod movement will have to be reduced. Very little body movement is required and movement of the hands alone should be sufficient for this cast.

The length of fly-line is then gradually increased and adjustments to hand and arm movements will be required to maintain the straight-line path and narrow loops. A pause will now be required, at the end of both the forward and back casts, to allow the fly-line to unroll.

As the fly rod flexes it will be found that the loop shape can be improved by bringing the casting movement to an abrupt stop. Also starting off the cast slowly and speeding up to the stop will help with loop formation.

Experiment

See what happens when insufficient rod movement is used. This will result in the fly-line tip tangling up with the belly of the fly line, causing a 'tailing loop'. But excessive movement of the fly rod will cause the loops to open and so the flight of the fly-line will not be as good and it will be difficult to cast in a moderate wind.

As the length of fly-line is increased, the stance will also have to be adjusted to allow for greater body movements to be made. The hands, arms and body will all have to be employed to keep the fly-line aerialised and to maintain good loops.

Tips for the overhead cast

- Slow down the tempo of the forward and back casts down until the fly-line almost collapses and begin the casting stroke very slowly, increasing to maximum rod-tip speed at the end of the casting stroke.

- Use shoulder, elbow and wrist pivots in sequence to increase the rod tip speed. Use the bottom hand for applying force and the top hand as a pivot when using a double-handed fly-rod. Concentrate on using the flexing of the fly-rod to cast the fly-line.

- Observe the fly-line as it rolls out and try to eliminate any tracking issues, or ripple in the aerialised fly-line. Try to get the loop as symmetrical and narrow as possible.

- Always maintain a straight-line path with the rod-tip, which will mean stopping the rod-tip abruptly, high, on the straight-line, at the end of the casting stroke.

- Try not to bend the wrist whilst casting a single-handed fly-rod because this will prevent the fly-rod from flexing.

Overhead forward cast (double-handed)

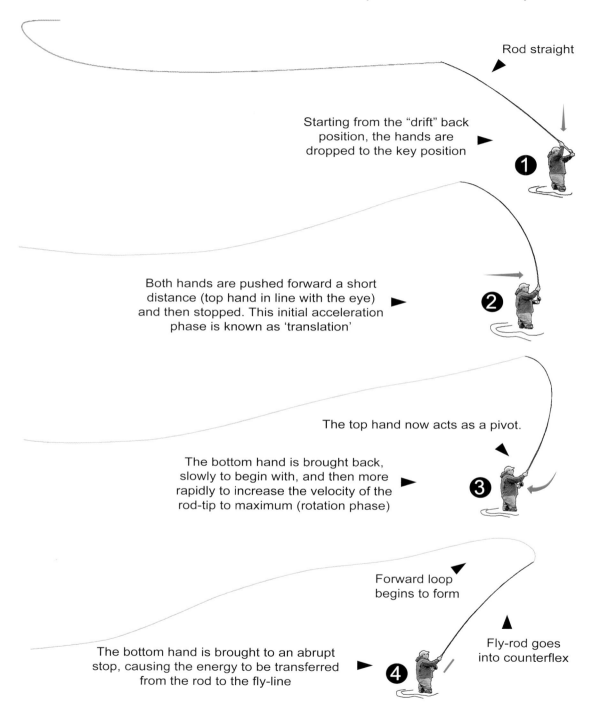

Rod straight

Starting from the "drift" back
position, the hands are
dropped to the key position

1

Both hands are pushed forward a short
distance (top hand in line with the eye)
and then stopped. This initial acceleration
phase is known as 'translation'

2

The top hand now acts as a pivot.

The bottom hand is brought back,
slowly to begin with, and then more
rapidly to increase the velocity of the
rod-tip to maximum (rotation phase)

3

Forward loop
begins to form

Fly-rod goes
into counterflex

The bottom hand is brought to an abrupt
stop, causing the energy to be transferred
from the rod to the fly-line

4

Overhead back cast (double-handed)

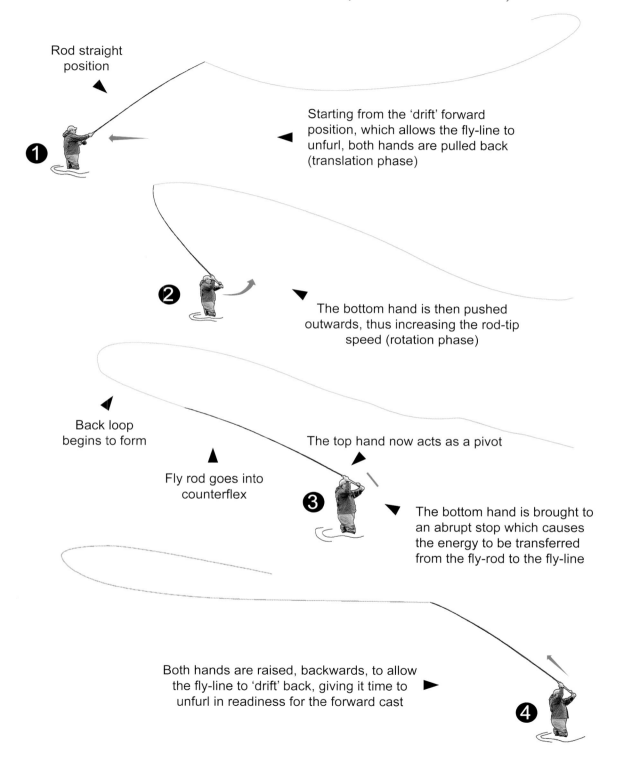

Rod straight
position

1

Starting from the 'drift' forward
position, which allows the fly-line to
unfurl, both hands are pulled back
(translation phase)

2

The bottom hand is then pushed
outwards, thus increasing the rod-tip
speed (rotation phase)

Back loop
begins to form

Fly rod goes into
counterflex

The top hand now acts as a pivot

3

The bottom hand is brought to
an abrupt stop which causes
the energy to be transferred
from the fly-rod to the fly-line

Both hands are raised, backwards, to allow
the fly-line to 'drift' back, giving it time to
unfurl in readiness for the forward cast

4

Overhead forward cast (single-handed)

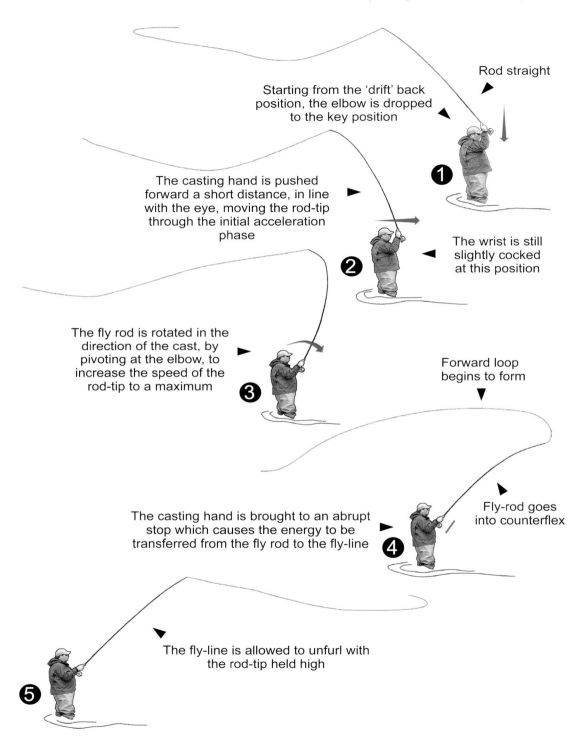

Rod straight

Starting from the 'drift' back position, the elbow is dropped to the key position

❶

The casting hand is pushed forward a short distance, in line with the eye, moving the rod-tip through the initial acceleration phase

❷

The wrist is still slightly cocked at this position

The fly rod is rotated in the direction of the cast, by pivoting at the elbow, to increase the speed of the rod-tip to a maximum

❸

Forward loop begins to form

The casting hand is brought to an abrupt stop which causes the energy to be transferred from the fly rod to the fly-line

❹

Fly-rod goes into counterflex

The fly-line is allowed to unfurl with the rod-tip held high

❺

Overhead back cast (single-handed)

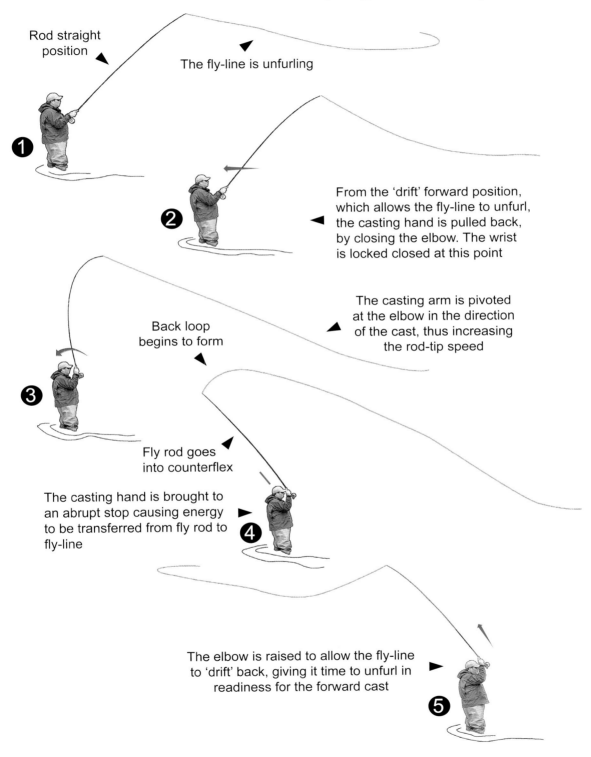

Rod straight position

The fly-line is unfurling

1

2

From the 'drift' forward position, which allows the fly-line to unfurl, the casting hand is pulled back, by closing the elbow. The wrist is locked closed at this point

The casting arm is pivoted at the elbow in the direction of the cast, thus increasing the rod-tip speed

Back loop begins to form

3

Fly rod goes into counterflex

The casting hand is brought to an abrupt stop causing energy to be transferred from fly rod to fly-line

4

The elbow is raised to allow the fly-line to 'drift' back, giving it time to unfurl in readiness for the forward cast

5

Static roll cast (single-handed)

When to use it

The static roll cast can be used to:

1. Straighten out a fly line after it has been stripped off the reel or before casting.
2. Cast a line when there is not room to make a back-cast.
3. Lift a dry-fly off the water, without disturbance.
4. Raise a sunken line and heavy fly before making a normal cast.
5. Set the hook when there is no room to strike.
6. Release flies that are caught in trees or undergrowth.
7. Learn the basic principles of Spey casting.

Problem Solving

When there's a strong downstream wind
Tilt the rod back further, until it touches the water if necessary, to ensure that a sufficiently large D-loop is formed.

If the forward cast is not going out
Try lifting the casting hand higher to make a bigger D-loop, thus pulling the anchor further back. Also, use a longer casting stroke.

If your cast plummets into the water
This indicates your 'stop' is too late in the forward cast.

Background notes to the method

3 The rod is inclined backwards forming a D-loop in the fly-line and creating a water-anchor. The latter is created by the resistance of the surface tension.

4 Lifting the rod higher and not changing its angle of incline has the effect of creating an even bigger D-loop, and pulling the anchor back helps with rod-loading when the forward cast is made.

5 Pushing the rod forward has the effect of pre-loading the rod. At the end of this forward movement (known as 'translation') the rod follows the casting plane and is then brought to an abrupt stop causing the energy to be transferred rapidly from rod to fly-line.

It is important that the rod-tip is stopped as close to the straight-line path as possible if a tight forward loop is to be created.

An upstream wind will assist in creating the D-loop.

Should the forward loop cross over and tangle with the line-tip this is because the casting line was not *inside* the anchor line.

The roll cast can also be used with a sinking line to bring it up to the surface before casting as normal.

Tips for the Static Roll Cast

- This cast requires a lot less effort and a lot less power stroke than imagined.

- Execute the cast slowly – there is no need to hurry.

- It is important to stop the rod-tip high, close to the straight-line path and to make the casting stroke as long as possible.

- The success of this cast depends on the formation of a good D-loop with an anchor as far back as possible and this can be checked very easily out of the corner of the eye before the cast is made.

- Always cast *inside* the anchor to prevent cross-over.

Static roll cast (single-handed)

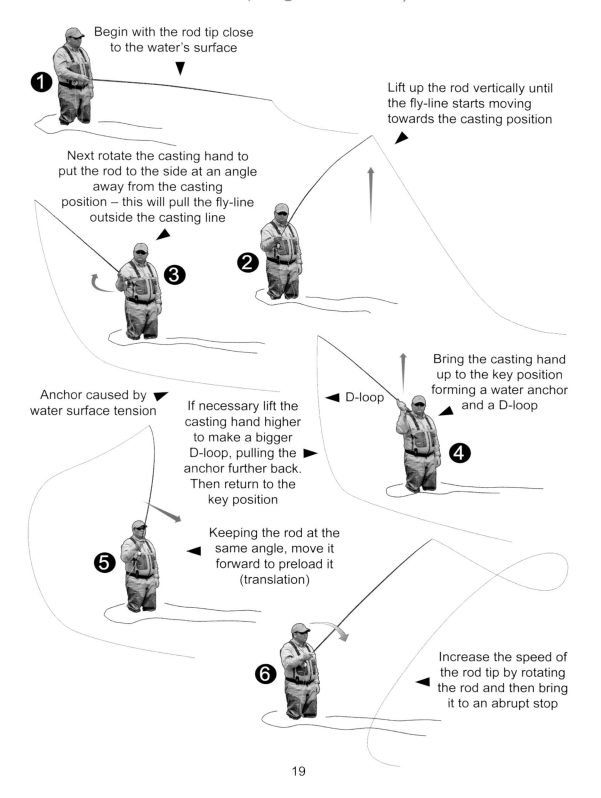

Begin with the rod tip close to the water's surface

Lift up the rod vertically until the fly-line starts moving towards the casting position

Next rotate the casting hand to put the rod to the side at an angle away from the casting position – this will pull the fly-line outside the casting line

Bring the casting hand up to the key position forming a water anchor and a D-loop

D-loop

Anchor caused by water surface tension

If necessary lift the casting hand higher to make a bigger D-loop, pulling the anchor further back. Then return to the key position

Keeping the rod at the same angle, move it forward to preload it (translation)

Increase the speed of the rod tip by rotating the rod and then bring it to an abrupt stop

Static roll cast Double-handed (set-up)

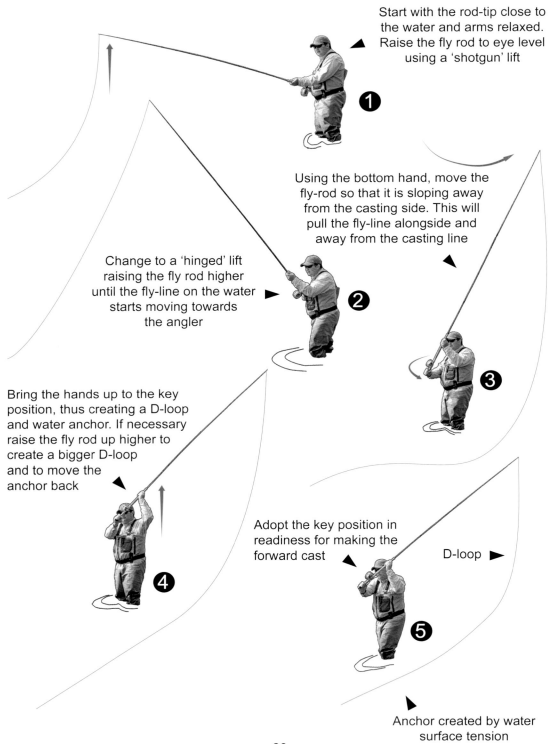

Start with the rod-tip close to the water and arms relaxed. Raise the fly rod to eye level using a 'shotgun' lift

❶

Using the bottom hand, move the fly-rod so that it is sloping away from the casting side. This will pull the fly-line alongside and away from the casting line

Change to a 'hinged' lift raising the fly rod higher until the fly-line on the water starts moving towards the angler

❷

❸

Bring the hands up to the key position, thus creating a D-loop and water anchor. If necessary raise the fly rod up higher to create a bigger D-loop and to move the anchor back

❹

Adopt the key position in readiness for making the forward cast

D-loop ▶

❺

Anchor created by water surface tension

20

Static roll cast Double-handed (forward cast)

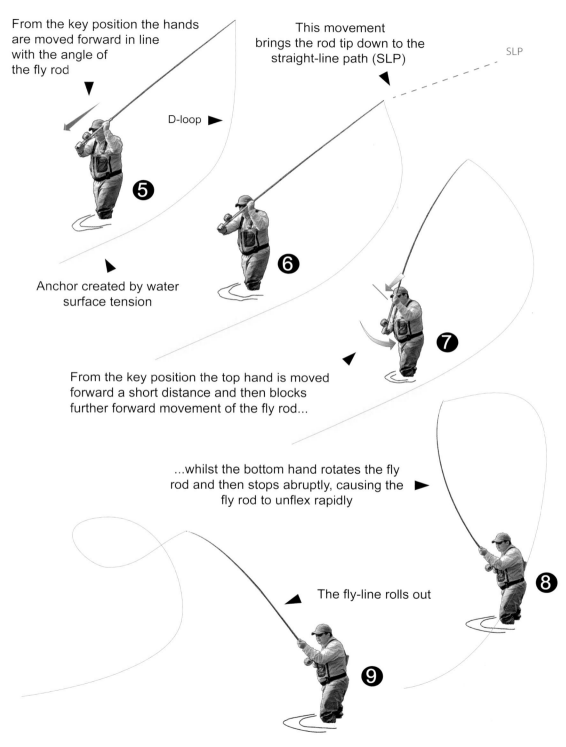

From the key position the hands are moved forward in line with the angle of the fly rod

This movement brings the rod tip down to the straight-line path (SLP)

SLP

D-loop ▶

❺

Anchor created by water surface tension

❻

From the key position the top hand is moved forward a short distance and then blocks further forward movement of the fly rod...

❼

...whilst the bottom hand rotates the fly rod and then stops abruptly, causing the fly rod to unflex rapidly ▶

The fly-line rolls out

❽

❾

Spey casting

Why Spey cast?

- When there is a need to change direction sharply between the downstream fly-line and the forward cast. The simple overhead cast is usually inadequate because it affords at most a 30° change to the casting angle: the Spey can do more.

- Spey casting is all about setting up the fly-line so that it is in the correct position to make the anchor, the back loop and, finally, the forward cast.

The diagram *(opposite)* shows a bird's eye view of river with a fisher using a double-handed fly-rod, in different casting situations, determined by the wind direction and the closest river bank.

By convention, right and left-hand banks apply when looking downstream.

The diagram illustrates how the fisher must be adept at casting from both the left-hand and right-hand sides of the body in order to be able to cast efficiently under all conditions and to make sure that the fly is always upwind, so that it cannot cause injury.

The single Spey cast applies for all wind directions **except a downstream wind**. For an upstream wind there are two other Spey casts that can be employed: the circle and the snap T. For a downstream wind, the double Spey or the snake roll casts can be used. Explanations of how to carry out each of these casts can be found in this book.

The diagram *(opposite, bottom)* shows some of the imaginary reference lines that are used by the Spey caster and these are adjusted depending on the position of the target, bank location (right or left-hand) and wind direction.

The **lift line** is normally where the fly-line comes to rest after it has finished swinging across the river and is sometimes called the '**dangle**'.

In all Spey casts the sequence is as follows:

1) Align your body with the target, in readiness for the final delivery.

2) After fishing out the previous cast the fly-line should be straightened out, downstream of the caster. If it isn't then this can be achieved by either making a roll cast or simply pulling in some fly-line.

3) The fly-line is now ready for lifting and further manipulation so that it is set-up for the forward cast (ie. by positioning an anchor and forming a D-loop).

4) The anchor should be positioned 1–1½ fly-rod's distance off the casting shoulder with the fly-line tip outside the casting line when the forward cast is made. Failure to do this will cause the fly-line to tangle with itself or the caster.

5) The anchor should be placed downwind of the casting-line so that the fly is in a safe position when the cast is made (the wind will then blow the fly away from the caster). Additional movements of the fly-line may be required for setting up the cast. Variations of the Spey cast are required to achieve this.

6) A D-loop must be formed behind the caster at 180 degrees opposite to the casting line. The D-loop will be on the downwind side of the caster.

7) The forward cast causes the fly-line to shoot out horizontally, from where it can drop onto the water in a straight line.

Spey casting reference lines

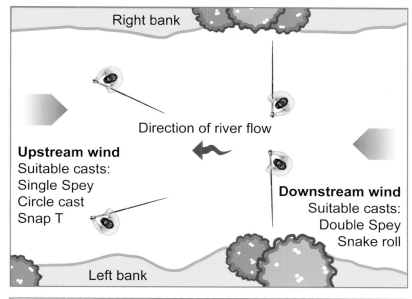

Right bank

Direction of river flow

Upstream wind
Suitable casts:
Single Spey
Circle cast
Snap T

Downstream wind
Suitable casts:
Double Spey
Snake roll

Left bank

Left: The various casting positions in the river and the casts which can be used depending upon the wind direction. Note the change of top hand, depending on wind direction.

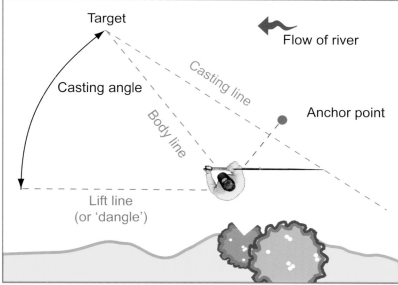

Target

Flow of river

Casting angle

Casting line

Body line

Anchor point

Lift line
(or 'dangle')

Left: The reference lines that are used in this book to help describe Spey casts.

The **casting angle** is the change of direction of the cast. Salmon fishers often cast at 30°–45° downstream, but sometimes they cast square at 90° when there is a slow current and the fly is required to move quicker. However, the important thing is that the caster always faces with his feet pointing in the general direction of the target. The upper body may rotate to face along the lift line but the feet remain in position.

It is essential that the water anchor is outside the casting line, otherwise the belly of the fly-line will pass over the line tip and cause it to tangle. This is why the recommended position of the anchor is a distance of 1–1½ fly-rod's length off the casting shoulder.

Jump roll cast (double-handed)

The jump roll cast is not a very useful fishing cast because the fly-line is cast back to where it came from. Nevertheless it is useful for demonstrating the basic essentials of Spey casting.

To begin with the caster faces his target, standing in a relaxed position, arms hanging down with the fly-rod just resting in the hands and the rod tip just above the surface of the water, with the fly-line out straight, downstream [1]. The fly-rod is then raised slightly in 'shotgun' style and pulled to the top hand side of the body. Pushing with the bottom hand will cause the fly-rod to flex against the resistance caused by water tension on the fly-line [2]. When it can hold it no longer, the rod will unflex and propel the fly-line back to the anchor position. The point at which the anchor lands is determined by the amount of pull applied by the top hand. It should be just over one rod length distance off the casting shoulder and slightly forward of the caster.

Once the fly-line has been released from the hold of the water tension, the fly-rod is allowed to track back, using both hands, until it passes over the anchor position [3]. At this moment the top hand circles up and the bottom hand is pushed forward, causing the fly-line to be thrown backwards in a big D-loop [4] and the fly-line to land gracefully on the water. The incline at which the rod-tip is brought back, the amount of circling up and push with the bottom hand will determine the shape of the loop, which in some circumstances may be V- rather than D-shaped.

A jump roll is a continuous motion cast. There is no pause to allow the D-loop to form, but the tempo is slowed down during this phase, which allows time for the hands to come up to the key position in readiness for the forward cast.

The forward cast is completed by moving the top hand forward about 6 inches (150mm) and level with the eye, closely followed by a slow pull with the bottom hand, rapidly quickening before being brought to an abrupt stop. The speed at which the final pull is applied will determine the amount of rod loading, and the abruptness of the stop will concentrate the energy transferred from fly rod to fly-line and consequently the tightness of the forward loop.

Tips for the double-handed jump roll cast

- As the fly-line breaks free of the water tension during the lift, maintain a *steady* tension but do not accelerate the rod tip.

- Even though this is a continuous cast it is a good idea to break it down into various stages such as lift, incline and anchor positioning. When these are familiar, practice circling up into the key position before making the forward cast.

- Practice lifting with various speeds and inclines until the optimum anchor position is found.

- Always cast inside the anchor line.

Jump roll cast (double-handed)

Start with the arms hanging from the side of the body, in a relaxed position, and the fly rod close to the water then raise it slightly using a shotgun lift ▶

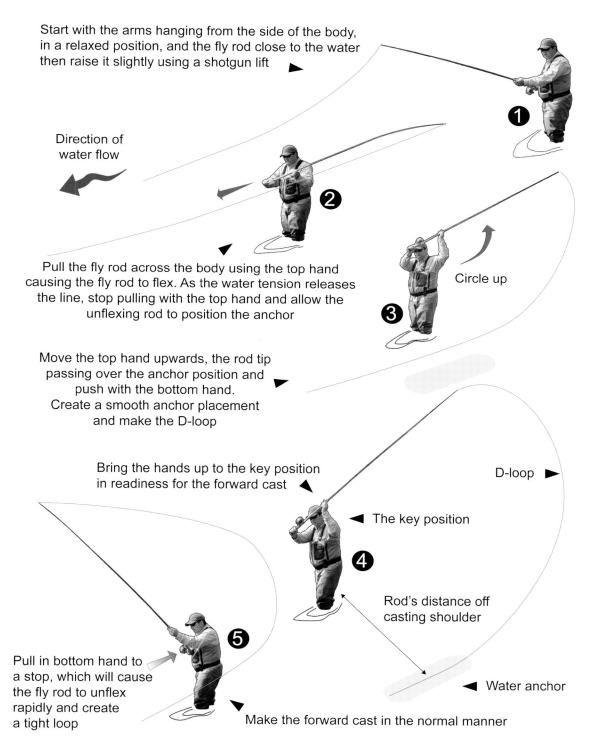

Direction of water flow

Pull the fly rod across the body using the top hand causing the fly rod to flex. As the water tension releases the line, stop pulling with the top hand and allow the unflexing rod to position the anchor

Circle up

Move the top hand upwards, the rod tip passing over the anchor position and push with the bottom hand. Create a smooth anchor placement and make the D-loop ▶

Bring the hands up to the key position in readiness for the forward cast ◀

D-loop ▶

◀ The key position

Rod's distance off casting shoulder

Pull in bottom hand to a stop, which will cause the fly rod to unflex rapidly and create a tight loop

◀ Water anchor

Make the forward cast in the normal manner

25

Jump roll cast (single-handed)

To begin the cast, stand in a relaxed position, with the fly-rod just resting in the hand, the rod-tip just above the surface of the water [1]. Then peel the fly-line off the water, pulling it up a shallow incline, with the fly rod to the side of the body [2]. Pulling backwards using the wrist will cause the fly-rod to flex because of the resistance caused by water tension on the fly-line, until it is unable to hold any longer.

At this moment the rod will unflex [3], propelling the fly-line back to the anchor position. The point at which the anchor lands will be determined by the amount of force that is applied though the fly rod.

Once the fly-line has been released from the hold of the water tension, the fly rod is swept backwards until it passes over the anchor position. The casting hand now circles up, causing the fly-line to be thrown backwards in a big D-loop [4]. The incline at which the rod tip is brought back and the amount of circling up of the casting hand will determine the shape of the loop. In some circumstances it may be V- rather than D-shaped.

A jump roll is a fluid cast and there should be no actual pause to allow the D-loop to form. However, the tempo *is* slowed down during this phase, allowing time for the casting hand to come up to the key position in readiness for the forward cast. The casting arm which has been used for the formation of the D-loop is now in the ideal position for making the forward cast [5].

The forward cast is completed by moving the casting hand forward, followed by a pivotal elbow rotation and a stop. The speed at which the rotation is applied will determine the amount of rod loading and the abruptness of the stop will concentrate the energy transferred from fly rod to the fly-line and consequently the tightness of the forward loop.

Jump roll visualisation diagram

Jump roll viewed from the side

Jump roll viewed from above

a) The fly-rod starts close to the water. b) As the fly-line starts to be drawn back towards the caster, sweep the fly-rod back up an inclined path. c) Circle up as the rod-tip passes over the anchor position d) Make the forward cast.

Jump roll cast (single-handed)

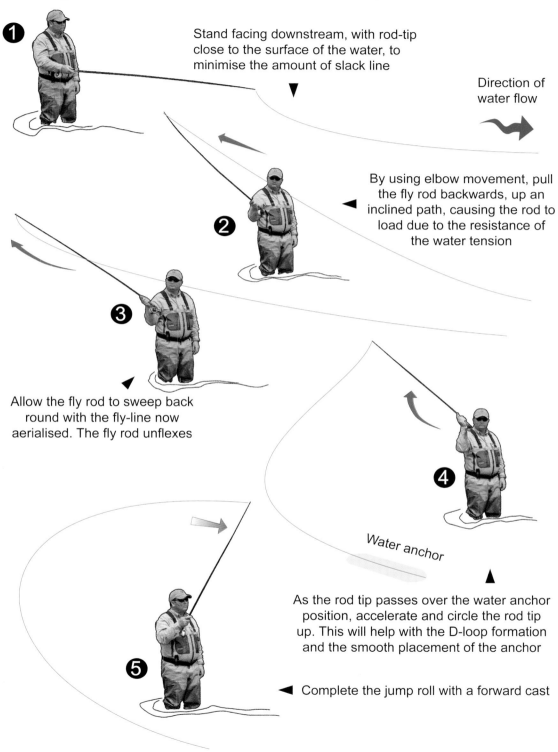

❶ Stand facing downstream, with rod-tip close to the surface of the water, to minimise the amount of slack line

Direction of water flow

❷ By using elbow movement, pull the fly rod backwards, up an inclined path, causing the rod to load due to the resistance of the water tension

❸ Allow the fly rod to sweep back round with the fly-line now aerialised. The fly rod unflexes

❹ As the rod tip passes over the water anchor position, accelerate and circle the rod tip up. This will help with the D-loop formation and the smooth placement of the anchor

Water anchor

❺ Complete the jump roll with a forward cast

Anchors

In Spey casting, the surface tension of the water is used to hold the fly-line (anchor) at the bottom of the D-loop. This assists in loading the fly rod during the forward cast. In the same way the surface tension anchors the fly-line during the initial lift before setting up a Spey cast.

Airborne v waterborne anchors

Some casts, such as the single Spey and snake roll, employ an anchor which is created by lifting the fly-line into the air (an **airborne anchor**), whereas other casts, such as the snap T and double Spey use an anchor which is created by laying the fly-line on the water and peeling it back off again (a **waterborne anchor**).

Anchor positioning

The efficiency of a Spey cast depends on anchor positioning and length. Ideally the tip of the fly-line should be just over a rod length out from the casting shoulder, with a length of fly-line on the water that is just adequate to hold the D-loop. Sometimes there is inadequate clearance behind the casting position to achieve correct positioning of the anchor and so it has to be placed further forward to the detriment of the D-loop shape.

With an airborne anchor it is essential to circle the rod tip up, as the anchor is formed. By doing this the fly-line will land smoothly on the water, rather than crashing down, which is a common casting fault, known as a **piled anchor**. The circling-up motion also assists with D-loop formation. In all of the casts, you need to have the anchor sliding back as the forward cast is started.

Common faults

Putting too much power into the anchor set-up cast (the back cast) will cause the anchor to skip and so it will be ineffective and the D-loop will not form correctly, thus making the forward cast difficult to achieve.

Having the anchor point too far downstream or upstream will cause an L shape (known as a **bloody L**) to form and this will also impair the forward cast. The key requirements for a forward cast are that the D-loop and anchor must be completely in line with the forward casting line. Excessive body rotation during a single Spey cast will also cause a bloody L to form.

If the anchor is too close to the casting position and inside the direction line of the forward cast then the fly-line will tangle. Making the forward

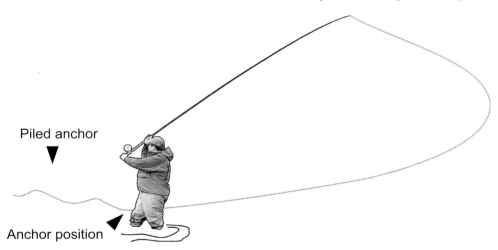

Piled anchor

Anchor position

This diagram shows a piled anchor, caused by dipping the rod tip as it is swept back, or by not circling up to form the D-loop. This is invariably formed too far downstream from the ideal anchor point.

Anchors – common faults

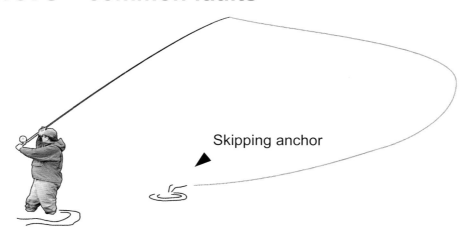

Skipping anchor

This diagram shows a skipping anchor, which occurs upstream of the proper anchor point, and is caused by putting too much power into the backcast.

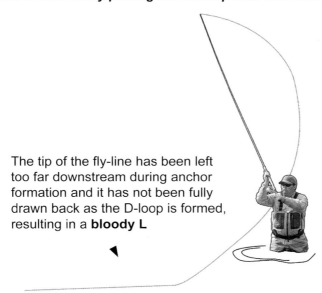

The tip of the fly-line has been left too far downstream during anchor formation and it has not been fully drawn back as the D-loop is formed, resulting in a **bloody L**

This shows a bloody L in an anchor, which means that it is not lined up in the direction of the cast (even though the D-loop itself may be). This causes an excessive amount of line stick and inhibits the forward cast.

cast too early, before the anchor has been formed, will cause the line tip to make a whip-cracking noise as it breaks the sound barrier.

The D-loop is used in all Spey casts and it provides a way of loading the fly rod and storing the fly-line in readiness for the forward cast. The main objective in all Spey casts is to set

up the fly-line in order to make this essential D-loop. The D-loop is a term that graphically describes the loop of fly-line, shaped like a letter 'D' (with the rod making the upright part), between the rod tip in the air and the line-tip on the water. It is created by moving the rod-tip backwards in an ascending path, with the

Anchors – common faults

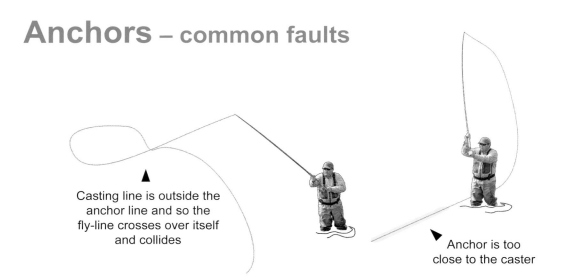

Casting line is outside the anchor line and so the fly-line crosses over itself and collides

Anchor is too close to the caster

The diagram above shows that by having an anchor that is too close to the body, and inside the casting line causes cross-over and a collision of the belly with the fly-line tip.

line-tip 'anchored' in the water. The D-loop line should be exactly 180° opposite the direction of the forward cast, looking from above.

Failure to raise and accelerate the rod tip backwards will create problems in forming the D-loop, especially when a long fly-line is used. Invariably this will cause problems with the forward cast because the fly rod will not be fully loaded, or there may be too much 'line stick'.

D-loop size is limited by fly rod length and the ability of the caster. However, it is possible to increase the fly rod loading by creating a more dynamic **V-loop** (see diagram opposite below).

It is preferable to make a D-loop when there is limited space for a back-cast. Here the rod-tip is lifted high and the D-loop is created with a nice, gentle, sweeping movement, with the emphasis on a high circling-up action.

However, if back space is not a problem, then the cast can be made much more efficiently, and with more energy, by creating a V-loop, which is achieved by sweeping the rod tip back low and up a very shallow incline and by pushing the line back using the bottom hand in the case of a two-handed fly-rod.

Tips for creating a good anchor and D-loop

- The D- or V-loop, anchor and fly-line must always line up with the casting line and the target.

- When the fly-rod is swept back to form a D-loop, the rod tip must always follow an inclined path otherwise the fly-line will be dumped on the water or it will pile.

- A splashy anchor indicates that the caster has not 'circled up' as the line-tip passes over the anchor point.

- Always allow sufficient time for the D-loop to form and observe it from the corner of the eye.

- Look at where the anchor is being set, not at the fly-line which is being lifted.

- Allow the fly rod to place the anchor, rather than using excessive arm and body movement.

The D-loop

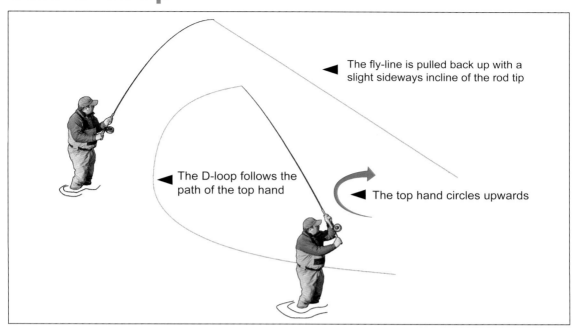

The fly-line is pulled back up with a slight sideways incline of the rod tip

The D-loop follows the path of the top hand

The top hand circles upwards

The V-loop

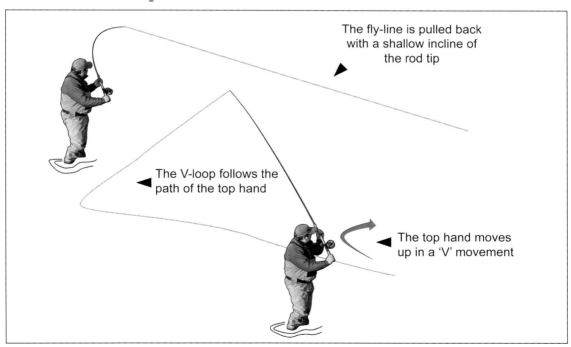

The fly-line is pulled back with a shallow incline of the rod tip

The V-loop follows the path of the top hand

The top hand moves up in a 'V' movement

The two diagrams above show the differences between the D-loop and the more dynamic V-loop. Both are determined by the angle of the lift and the top hand movement.

Single Spey cast (double-handed)

This is a useful cast for when there is an upstream wind.

The single Spey cast moves the fly from a downstream position to across the river, changing direction up to 90 degrees. An anchor and hence the fly are placed upstream of the casting position for safety and the fly is thus blown away from the caster.

When fishing from the right hand bank, the left hand is uppermost and when fishing from the left hand bank, the right hand is uppermost.

Place your feet so that your body is facing in the direction of the forward cast (for stability and comfort one foot may point slightly downstream whilst the other points across stream). The upper body should then be turned to face downstream, arms hanging in a relaxed manner, and this will dictate the position of the hands on the butt of the fly rod. The rod tip should be close to the surface of the water so that there is no slack in the fly-line.

The first move [1] involves lifting and slowly sweeping the fly rod in towards the bank, which will increase the impetus of the fly-line when it is swept back again and it will also help to lift the fly-line as it is peeled off the water. The in-swing also increases sweep length when the fly-line is aerialised and helps to achieve good anchor placement. The bottom hand should be used to manipulate the rod for the sweep into the river bank. After this preparatory sweep, the bottom hand is again used to change direction of the sweep out into midstream [2]. The force used will load the fly rod and then propel the fly-line as the line tip is released from the water.

Rotating the body round to the forward casting position [3], continue to sweep the rod tip round until it is over the anchor point [4] and then push forward with the bottom hand, whilst circling up with the top hand and in so doing a large D-loop will be formed [5]. The tempo of the cast should be slowed at this point to allow the D-loop to form fully, and the fly rod is loaded in readiness for the forward cast.

The success of this cast depends on the initial sweep into the bank, followed by the wide sweep around across the river – no shortcuts! The main function of the top hand is to circle up, to create a smooth, controlled, positioning of the anchor and a nice full D-loop.

Tips for the double-handed single Spey cast

- Peel the fly-line off the water during the in-swing and continue to do so during the initial part of the out-swing. Rotating your body as the water tension releases the fly-line will help you perfect this cast.

- Swinging the rod towards the bank (the in-swing) helps to lift the fly-line off the water.

- Make sure that your feet are facing the target and that your upper body rotates from the initial lift to anchor placement.

- Ensure that the casting hand (top-hand) circles up and that the fly rod is pulled right back to the key position.

- Practice the jump roll until it becomes second nature and then introduce body rotation, starting with a small change of direction and increasing gradually. Next, introduce the in-swing towards your own bank, to achieve a greater change of direction.

Single Spey cast (double-handed)

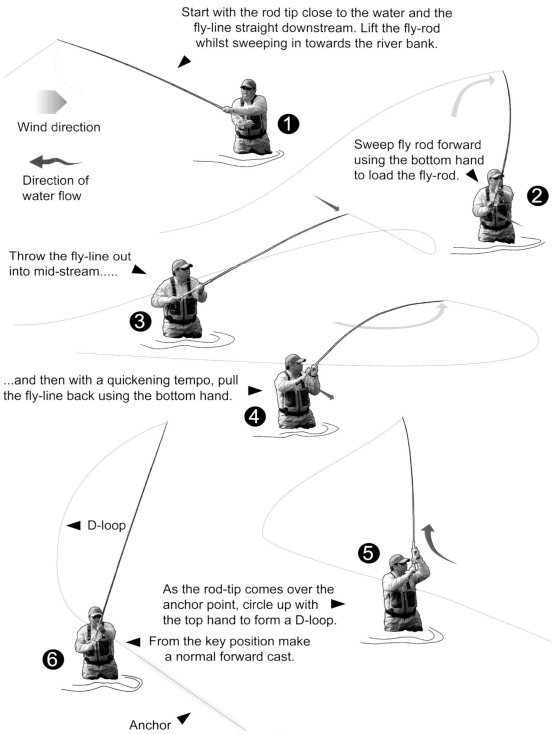

Start with the rod tip close to the water and the fly-line straight downstream. Lift the fly-rod whilst sweeping in towards the river bank.

❶

Wind direction

Direction of water flow

Sweep fly rod forward using the bottom hand to load the fly-rod. ◄

❷

Throw the fly-line out into mid-stream..... ►

❸

...and then with a quickening tempo, pull the fly-line back using the bottom hand. ►

❹

❺

D-loop ◄

As the rod-tip comes over the anchor point, circle up with ► the top hand to form a D-loop.

From the key position make ◄ a normal forward cast.

❻

Anchor ▼

33

Single Spey cast (single-handed)

When fishing from the left hand bank, the right hand is used in the conventional manner for a right-handed caster but fishing from the left hand bank then it is necessary to cast across the body.

Face in the direction of the forward cast (for stability and comfort the one foot may be pointing slightly downstream whilst the other points across stream). The upper body should then be turned to face downstream and the casting arm should be hanging down in a relaxed manner. The rod tip should be close to the surface of the water so that there is no slack in the fly-line [1].

The first move involves lifting from the elbow and slowly sweeping the fly rod in towards the bank using your wrist [2]. The length of this initial back sweep is determined by the change of the direction angle. It will also help to lift the fly-line off the water. The in-swing also increases sweep length when the fly-line is aerialised and helps to achieve good anchor placement. After this preparatory sweep, the rod is moved in the opposite direction so that it sweeps out into midstream. The force used will load the fly rod and then carry the fly-line as the line tip is released from the water.

Rotating the body round to the forward casting position [3], continue to sweep the rod tip out and round until it is over the anchor point and then accelerate and circle up [4], by lifting the elbow, to form a D-loop. The tempo of the cast should then be slowed to allow the D-loop to form fully [5].

The success of this cast depends upon the initial sweep into the bank, followed by the wide sweep around across the river (no short cuts), the rapid acceleration of the fly rod backwards as the D-loop is formed, which also pulls the anchor back, and these are all achieved by manipulating the wrist.

Single Spey visualisation diagram

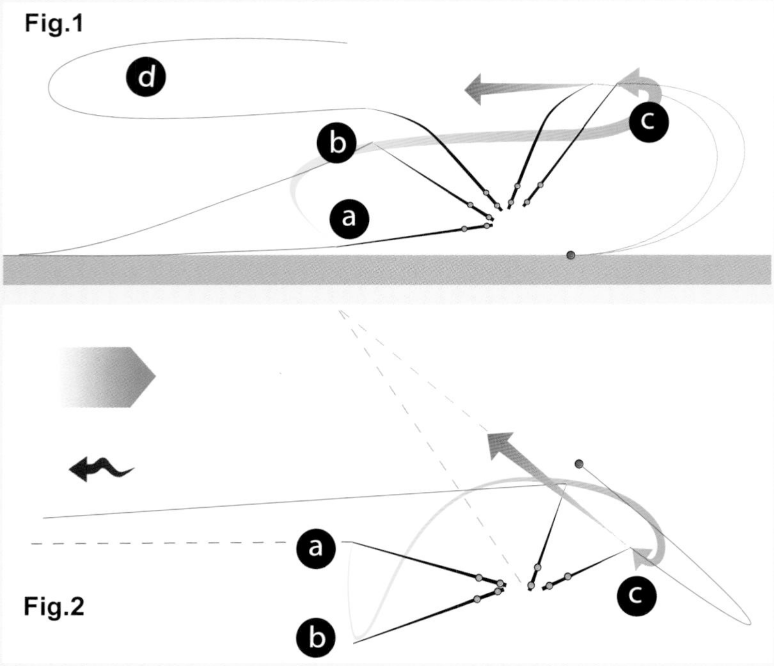

Fig.1

Fig.2

These two diagrams show a view of the cast from the side (Fig.1) and from above (Fig.2).

a) Start with the rod tip close to the water.

b) Lift the rod tip up and swing the fly rod in towards the bank.

c) Then sweep out and round, circling up as the rod tip passes over the anchor position.

d) Make the forward cast.

Single Spey cast (single-handed)

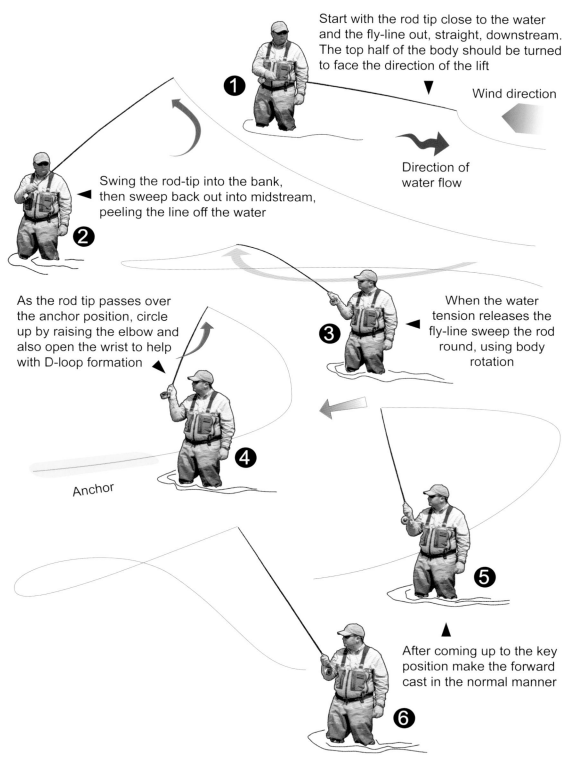

1 Start with the rod tip close to the water and the fly-line out, straight, downstream. The top half of the body should be turned to face the direction of the lift

Wind direction

Direction of water flow

2 Swing the rod-tip into the bank, then sweep back out into midstream, peeling the line off the water

3 When the water tension releases the fly-line sweep the rod round, using body rotation

4 As the rod tip passes over the anchor position, circle up by raising the elbow and also open the wrist to help with D-loop formation

Anchor

5 After coming up to the key position make the forward cast in the normal manner

6

Snap-T cast (double-handed)

When to use it

A Snap-T cast can be used when there is an upstream wind, primarily to keep the fly on the safe side of the body but also to take advantage of the wind which will help to carry the line outwards during the forward cast. A waterborne anchor is used to hold the fly-line as the cast is set up. This is one of the easiest casts for a beginner to learn and when done properly it looks impressive.

Unlike other Spey casts, it is not necessary to turn the upper body, to face downstream, in order to make this cast because it starts with the fly rod across the stream with the fly-line straight downstream [1]. The first move involves lifting the fly rod back [2] at an angle whilst keeping the line under steady tension. When most of the fly-line is off the water the direction of the fly rod is rapidly reversed, by 180 degrees, using a quick movement of the bottom hand, and the fly-line is cast down onto the water [3]. As a consequence the free end of the fly-line will flip over [4], upstream and form a waterborne anchor. The rod tip will end up close to the surface of the water.

Once all of the fly-line has settled on the water, the fly rod can be swept back upstream, with the rod tip following a slow inclined path [5], whilst steadily peeling the fly-line off the water and keeping the fly-line constantly under tension. As the rod tip passes over the forward anchor position [6], the top hand circles up and the bottom hand pushes back, to form a nice big D-loop. This will also have the effect of pulling the anchor back into position [7]. At the end of this sequence the hands will be in the key position, in readiness for the forward cast [8].

Snap-Z

A variation of this cast is called the Snap-Z. It is used with sunk lines and heavy flies and during the set up of the cast, after the initial lift, the rod is not flexed down so heavily, causing the fly-line to begin to turn over, back upstream, but it runs out of energy and falls on the water in a 'Z' shape – hence the name of the cast.

Tips for the double-handed Snap-T cast

- This cast was developed for use with short-head fly-lines and it works best with **shooting-heads** or **Skagit lines**.

- Be sure to tuck the rod tip under the fly-line during the downward snap.

- When practising, make as little a snap as possible - it is surprising how little effort is required to move the fly-line into the correct anchor position. This will also prevent flies from snapping off when fishing.

- For longer fly-lines, at the end of the snap, as the fly line is moving upstream, move the fly-rod in towards the bank, pulling the fly-line downstream, thus preventing a bloody L.

- During the set up, the angle of the lift and the "snap" down will determine where the end of the fly-line lands, so if there is a fast current, the angle should be shallower so that the fly line goes further back. When a long fly-line is used, the angle should be much steeper to prevent the line-tip from going too far upstream.

- When the cast is made across and downstream, at an angle rather than square, the lift is made in towards the river bank.

Snap-T cast (double-handed)

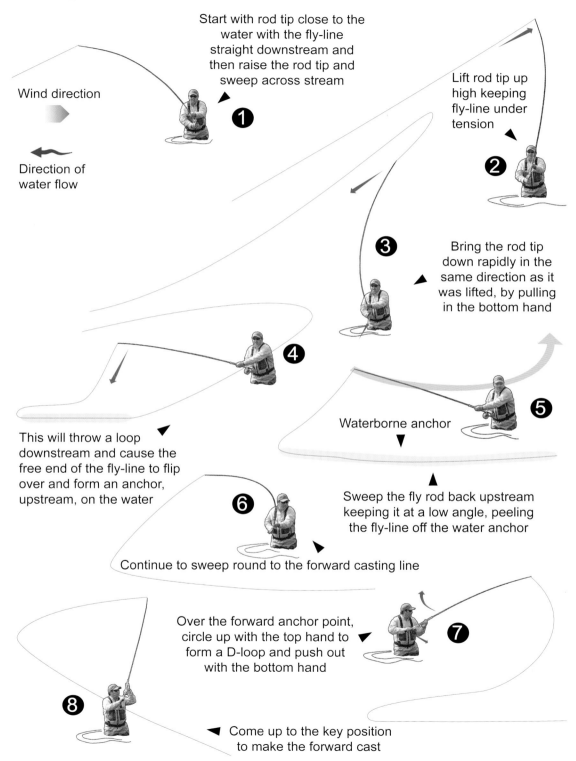

Start with rod tip close to the water with the fly-line straight downstream and then raise the rod tip and sweep across stream ❶

Wind direction

Direction of water flow

Lift rod tip up high keeping fly-line under tension ❷

❸

Bring the rod tip down rapidly in the same direction as it was lifted, by pulling in the bottom hand

❹

Waterborne anchor

❺

This will throw a loop downstream and cause the free end of the fly-line to flip over and form an anchor, upstream, on the water

❻

Sweep the fly rod back upstream keeping it at a low angle, peeling the fly-line off the water anchor

Continue to sweep round to the forward casting line

Over the forward anchor point, circle up with the top hand to form a D-loop and push out with the bottom hand ❼

❽

Come up to the key position to make the forward cast

Snap-T cast (single-handed)

The first move involves lifting the fly rod back at an angle whilst keeping the line under tension [**2**]. When most of the fly-line is off the water, the direction of the fly rod is rapidly reversed by 180 degrees [**3**] using a quick wrist movement, and the fly-line is cast down onto the water. The free end of the fly-line will flip over, upstream, and form a waterborne anchor. The rod tip should end up close to the surface of the water.

Once all of the fly-line has settled on the water [**4**], the fly rod can be swept back upstream, with the rod tip following a slow inclined path, whilst steadily peeling the fly-line off the water and keeping the fly-line constantly under tension [**5**]. As the rod tip passes over the forward anchor position, the casting hand circles up, to form a nice big D-loop [**6**]. This will also have the effect of pulling the anchor back into alignment. At the end of this sequence, the casting hand will be in the key position, in readiness for the forward cast.

Tips for the Snap-T cast

- The angle of the lift and the "snap" down will determine where the end of the fly-line lands and so when there is a fast current, the angle should be shallower so that the fly-line goes further back. When a long fly-line is used, the angle should be much steeper to prevent the line-tip from going too far upstream.

- When the cast is made across and downstream, at an angle rather than square, the lift is made in towards the river bank.

Snap-Z

There is another version of this cast which is called the Snap-Z – *see page 36*.

Snap-T visualisation diagram

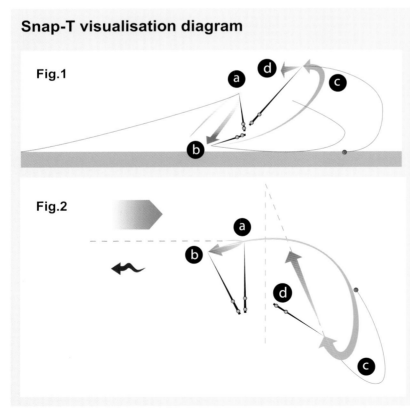

Fig.1

Fig.2

The two diagrams show a view of the cast from the side (Fig.1) and from above (Fig.2).

a) Start by lifting the rod and the fly-line off the water.

b) Snap the rod back down in the direction from where it was first lifted from. This will cause the fly-line to turn over, upstream, forming a waterborne anchor.

c) Then sweep out and round, circling up as the rod tip passes over the anchor position.

d) Make the forward cast.

Snap-T cast (single-handed)

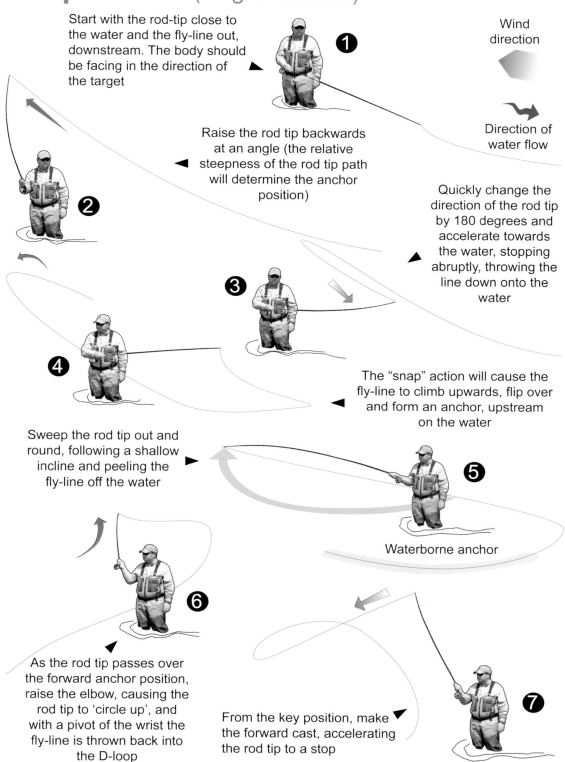

Start with the rod-tip close to the water and the fly-line out, downstream. The body should be facing in the direction of the target

❶

Wind direction

Raise the rod tip backwards at an angle (the relative steepness of the rod tip path will determine the anchor position)

Direction of water flow

Quickly change the direction of the rod tip by 180 degrees and accelerate towards the water, stopping abruptly, throwing the line down onto the water

❷

❸

❹

The "snap" action will cause the fly-line to climb upwards, flip over and form an anchor, upstream on the water

Sweep the rod tip out and round, following a shallow incline and peeling the fly-line off the water

❺

Waterborne anchor

❻

As the rod tip passes over the forward anchor position, raise the elbow, causing the rod tip to 'circle up', and with a pivot of the wrist the fly-line is thrown back into the D-loop

From the key position, make the forward cast, accelerating the rod tip to a stop

❼

Double Spey cast (double-handed)

The double Spey cast is used when there is a downstream wind, in order to keep the fly on the safe (downwind) side of the body. The wind assists in the formation of a D-loop and it carries the fly-line through the forward cast. A waterborne anchor is employed during the setting up sequence of this cast.

As with all Spey casts, your feet should point in the direction of the forward cast; the top half of your body will turn to face downstream. To begin with the rod tip is held close to the water, with the fly-line straight downstream and this is achieved by standing in a relaxed posture [1] with the hands holding the rod butt loosely.

Next, lift the rod tip vertically [2], sweep upstream, tracing a horizontal rod tip path [3], which will cause the fly-line to be aerialised, and then drop the rod tip vertically, whilst at the same time throwing an upstream loop on the water [4]. The size of the loop will determine the downstream anchor position and should be adjusted to compensate for a fast flowing current or a longer fly-line. It is important that the rod tip ends low, close to the water. Most of the line, outside the rod tip, will now be on the water and this will form the waterborne anchor.

The fly-line is then peeled off the water by sweeping back downstream and tracking a shallow inclined path with the rod tip. The speed at which the sweep is made ensures that the fly-line is always under tension as it is peeled off the water's surface. The wider the sweep, the better the resulting D-loop at the end of it. Continue the sweep until the rod tip passes over the forward cast anchor position [5] and at this moment circle up with the top hand to throw a big D-loop, whilst pushing with the bottom hand, to draw the fly-line back to the correct anchor position. The hands will now come up to the key position in readiness for the forward cast.

The bottom hand is dominant for most of this cast and so this means that the hands are crossed over when the waterborne anchor is made and the bottom hand is used to sweep the fly rod back round when the fly-line is being peeled off the water [6], finally pushing outwards to form a good D-loop. The top hand is used mainly for circling up. Often, not enough energy is put into the D-loop back cast and much of the line remains on the water. This causes the line to 'stick' as the forward cast is made [7]. It may also mean that the anchor is not pulled sufficiently back and lined up – resulting in a bloody L.

Tips for the Double-handed Spey cast

- Instead of looking at where the upstream loop is formed, pay attention to where the line-tip lands to ensure that it pulls round to 180° opposite the forward cast.

- At the start of the cast it is best to keep the fly-line as far away as possible, out in the river, because this will help to create greater rod loading, whilst sweeping round to the key position.

- Keep the rod tip close to the water's surface at the end of the upstream anchor formation - even touch the water with the rod tip if necessary.

- Peel the fly-line off the water, slowly at first, the rod tip moving up a low, inclined path. Accelerate as the D-loop forms.

- Allow a pause for the D-loop to fully form and look at it out of the corner of the eye to make sure that it has done so.

Double Spey cast (double-handed)

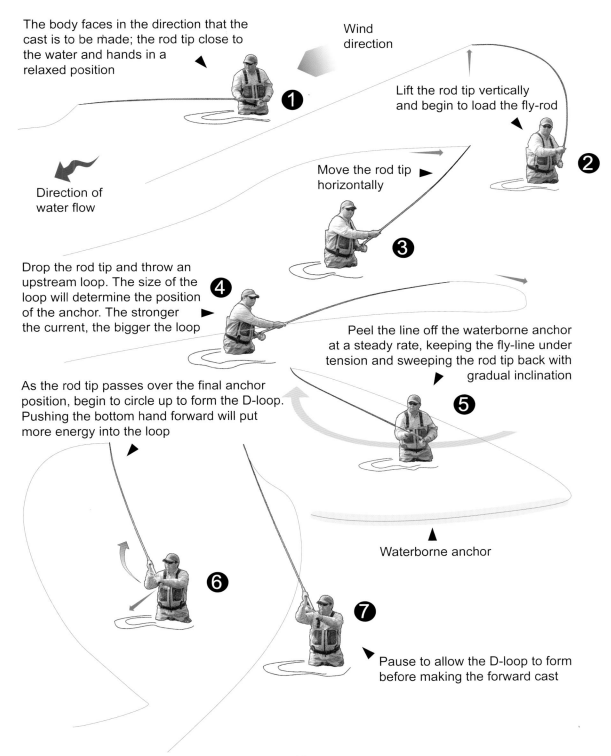

The body faces in the direction that the cast is to be made; the rod tip close to the water and hands in a relaxed position

①

Wind direction

Lift the rod tip vertically and begin to load the fly-rod

②

Move the rod tip horizontally

③

Direction of water flow

Drop the rod tip and throw an upstream loop. The size of the loop will determine the position of the anchor. The stronger the current, the bigger the loop

④

Peel the line off the waterborne anchor at a steady rate, keeping the fly-line under tension and sweeping the rod tip back with gradual inclination

⑤

As the rod tip passes over the final anchor position, begin to circle up to form the D-loop. Pushing the bottom hand forward will put more energy into the loop

Waterborne anchor

⑥

⑦

Pause to allow the D-loop to form before making the forward cast

Double Spey cast (single-handed)

Background notes to the method

The upstream loop
The size of the loop will determine the downstream anchor position and may be adjusted to compensate for a fast flowing current or a longer fly-line. It is important that the rod tip ends low, close to the water. Most of the line will now be on the water and this will form a waterborne anchor.

The sweep
The speed at which the sweep is made ensures that the fly-line is always under tension as it is peeled off the water's surface. The wider the sweep, the better the resulting D-loop at the end of it. Continue to sweep until the rod tip passes over the forward cast anchor position and at this moment circle up, by lifting the elbow, to throw a big D-loop, whilst using wrist action to draw the fly-line back to the correct anchor position. Ultimately, the hand will come up to the key position in readiness for the forward cast.

In the example (*page 43*) the forward cast [**Fig.7**] is made over the body and this may be necessary when casting from the left-bank side of the river. However the basic movements are the same for conventional casting as well. Rod-tip speed, for longer casting, can be increased by adding a haul to the forward cast.

Tips for the cast

- Contrary to intuition, this cast should not be hurried, especially during the formation of the waterborne anchor.

- It is best to look at the tip of the fly-line, rather than the upstream loop, to ensure that the anchor is placed in the correct position.

Double Spey visualisation diagram

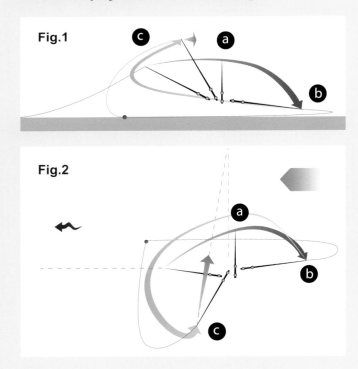

Fig.1

Fig.2

These two diagrams show a view of the cast from the side (Fig.1) and from above (Fig.2).

a) Lift the rod up and over.

b) Place the rod tip upstream, laying the fly-line on the water with the line tip in the anchor position.

c) Then sweep out and round downstream, up a shallow incline, circling up as the rod tip passes over the anchor position.

d) Make the forward cast.

Double Spey cast (single-handed)

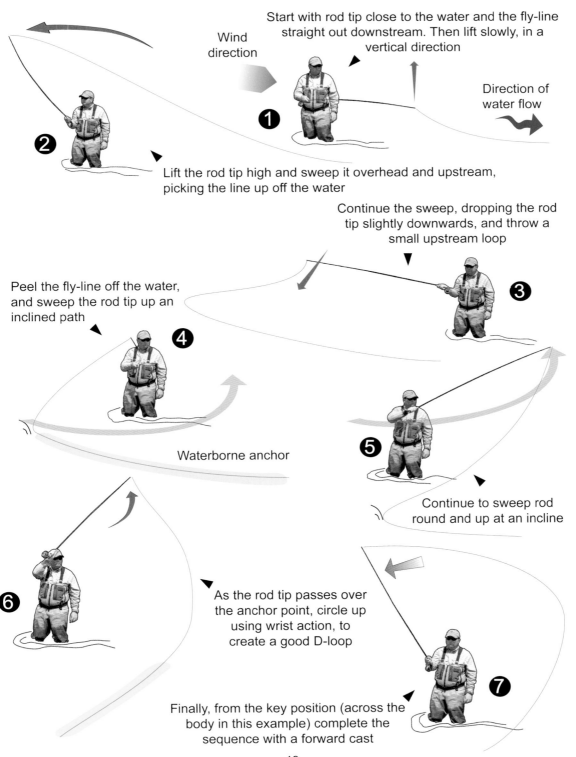

Wind direction

Start with rod tip close to the water and the fly-line straight out downstream. Then lift slowly, in a vertical direction

Direction of water flow

❶

❷

Lift the rod tip high and sweep it overhead and upstream, picking the line up off the water

Continue the sweep, dropping the rod tip slightly downwards, and throw a small upstream loop

❸

Peel the fly-line off the water, and sweep the rod tip up an inclined path

❹

Waterborne anchor

❺

Continue to sweep rod round and up at an incline

❻

As the rod tip passes over the anchor point, circle up using wrist action, to create a good D-loop

❼

Finally, from the key position (across the body in this example) complete the sequence with a forward cast

Snake roll cast (single-handed)

When to use it

A snake roll works most effectively when there is a downstream wind because this helps to pull the fly-line through the rod rings, making it sail out in an impressive fashion. The snake roll can also be used for repositioning the fly-line up or down stream.

Initially, the fly rod is lifted back in towards the bank (don't forget to face the target) and the rod tip is swept over the fly-line, throwing the belly of the fly-line forward and out towards the middle of the stream. The rod-tip is then tucked under the fly-line, following an elliptical, or rugby ball-shaped, path and brought back rapidly, pulling the line back with it. As the line-tip passes over the anchor point, the casting hand is circled up, and the fly rod is brought round and over, to create a large D-loop and provide a smooth landing of the fly-line on the water. The casting hand should finish in the key position ready to make the forward cast.

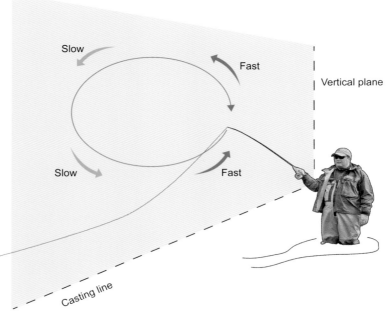

This cast is made by following an elliptical path of the rod tip in the same plane which has its base along the casting line

Slow

Fast

Vertical plane

Slow

Fast

Casting line

Tips for the Static Roll Cast

- This cast varies greatly in speed, otherwise the fly-line would splash down on the water. Punching the fly-line out, turning it over slowly and then pulling it back quickly will give the best result - it is almost as if there are two rapid out and in movements with a steady slow movement in-between.

- Use a rotational and sweeping arm action to throw the line back to make the D-loop and to pull the anchor back at the same time.

- Don't forget to circle up at the appropriate time because this will also help with a nice graceful anchor placement, instead of the fly-line crashing down.

- The wider the elliptical path of the rod tip, the more horizontal the returning fly-line.

- For beginners, a good way to remember this cast is to say 'bank-river-bank'.

Snake roll cast (single-handed)

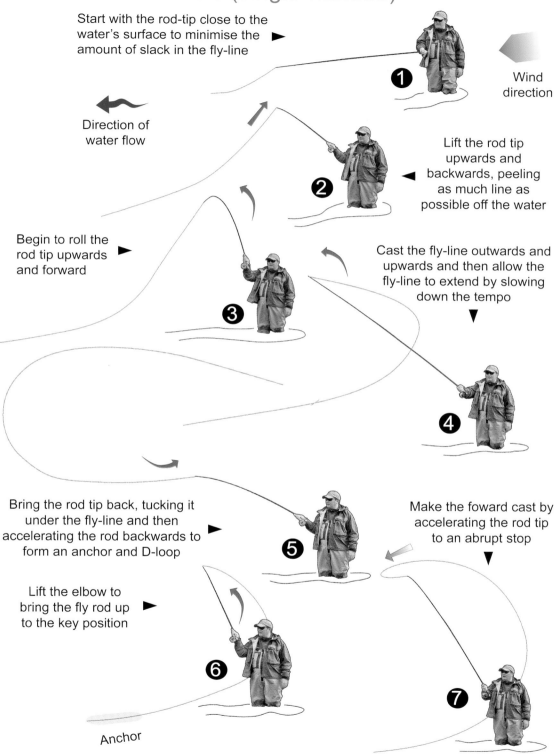

Start with the rod-tip close to the water's surface to minimise the amount of slack in the fly-line ►

❶

Wind direction

Direction of water flow

Lift the rod tip upwards and backwards, peeling as much line as possible off the water ◄

❷

Begin to roll the rod tip upwards and forward ►

Cast the fly-line outwards and upwards and then allow the fly-line to extend by slowing down the tempo ▼

❸

❹

Bring the rod tip back, tucking it under the fly-line and then accelerating the rod backwards to form an anchor and D-loop ►

Make the foward cast by accelerating the rod tip to an abrupt stop ▼

❺

Lift the elbow to bring the fly rod up to the key position ►

❻

❼

Anchor

Snake roll cast (double-handed)

Snake roll visualisation diagram

Fig.1

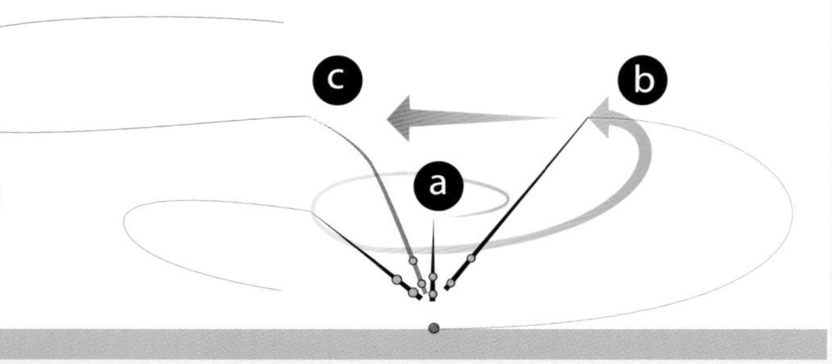

Fig.2

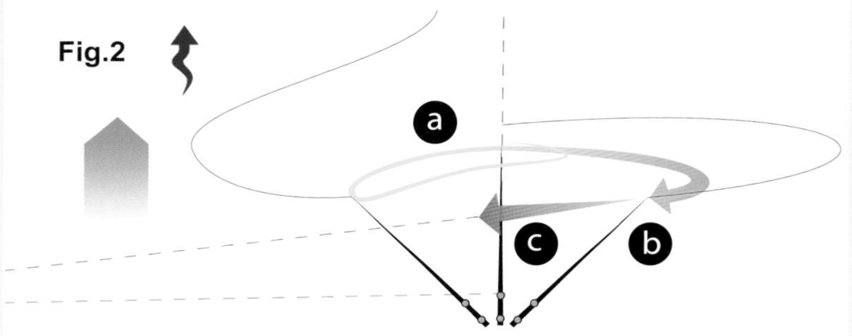

*These two diagrams show a view of the cast
from the side (Fig.1) and from above (Fig.2).*

*a) Start by lifting the rod and the fly-line off the water. Then
rotate the rod around an elliptical path by firstly moving the
rod tip backwards, upwards and then forwards, finally coming
back under the fly-line, causing it to flip over.*

*b) As the rod tip passes over the anchor point, circle up to the
key position.*

c) Make the forward cast.

Snake roll cast (double-handed)

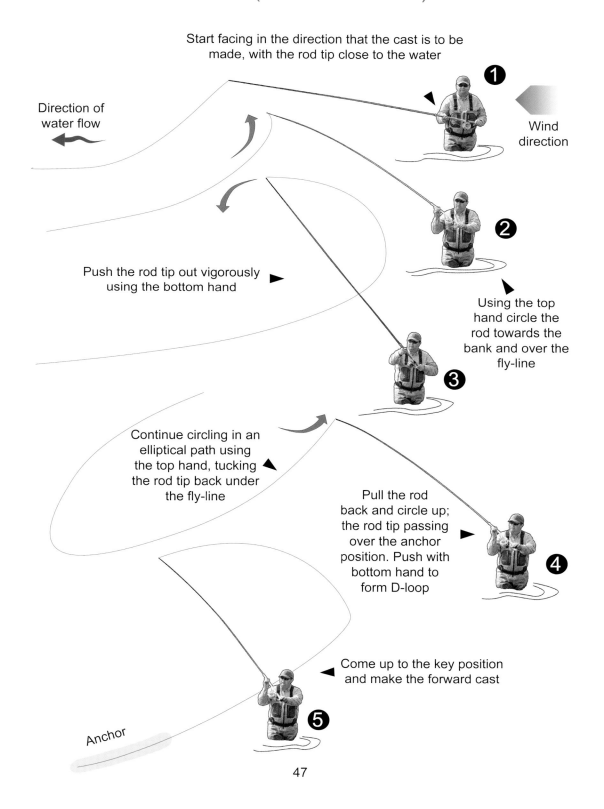

Start facing in the direction that the cast is to be made, with the rod tip close to the water

Direction of water flow

Wind direction

Push the rod tip out vigorously using the bottom hand

Using the top hand circle the rod towards the bank and over the fly-line

Continue circling in an elliptical path using the top hand, tucking the rod tip back under the fly-line

Pull the rod back and circle up; the rod tip passing over the anchor position. Push with bottom hand to form D-loop

Come up to the key position and make the forward cast

Anchor

Hauling

By introducing a haul into the cast, you will increase the line speed and also put a small amount of extra energy into the rod by creating more bending. This aerialises a longer fly-line and propels additional fly-line through the rings.

Hauling may be used during both the forward and back casts. This is referred to as **double-hauling**. It is also possible to cast into a strong wind using a **single-haul** because the wind itself will carry the fly-line in the other direction.

A haul is when the fly-line is pulled with the line hand in the opposite direction to that of the fly rod. The moment to apply the haul is at the end of the power stroke.

Hauls can also be used in roll and Spey casts to develop greater line speed and rod-energy.

As a first step, a single haul can be practised for either the front or back cast on grass. In between each cast, the fly-line can be laid down so that the student can focus on the haul itself without having to think about aerialising the line as well. The hands are held together for the translation phase and then the hauling hand is pulled away during the rotation phase, which is when the highest tip speed is achieved.

Unlike conventional casting, the rod hand does not accelerate to an abrupt stop but instead it slows down whilst the hauling hand is allowed to drift back to the rod hand, maintaining line tension all the time. The hauling hand will, in effect, be pulled back by the weight of the fly-line.

Tips for hauling

- For the back cast the fly-line is hauled outwards, in the opposite direction to which the fly-rod points *(see page 49)*.

- During the forward cast the fly-line is hauled downwards *(see page 49)*.

- It is best to pull the haul in line with the rod rings because this will reduce ring friction, and rod loading will be more efficient.

- The haul should not start until half-way through the casting stroke.

- The haul hand goes back to the casting hand, as the fly-line rolls out after the stop, gently maintaining tension on the fly-line.

- It is important to remember that a short length of line outside the rod tip requires a short haul and a long length of fly-line requires a long haul *(see also the section on LEAPS, page 79)*.

Hauling

Keeping both hands together accelerate the rod backwards using translation only (no rotation of the rod)

Then close the elbow to cause rod rotation and at the same time pull the line down in the opposite direction to that of the rod

Haul outwards

As the rod is allowed to drift back bring the line hand back up to meet the rod hand

To complete the power-stroke open the elbow to cause rod rotation and at the same time pull the line downwards

Now begin the forward cast keeping both hands together and accelerate the rod forwards using translation only (no rotation of the rod)

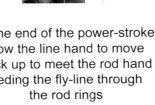

Haul downwards

At the end of the power-stroke allow the line hand to move back up to meet the rod hand feeding the fly-line through the rod rings

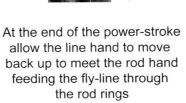

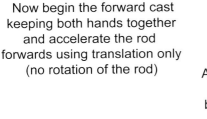

49

Other change-of-direction casts

There are a number of reasons why a fisher might want to cast in a different direction from the lift line: to cover a fish, to move the fly from downstream on the dangle to upstream or to systematically fish down and across a river.

Overhead casting is limited to an angle change of about 30°, whilst Spey casting offers a much broader range and for this reason is covered extensively in this book. However, there are other single-handed techniques that put the fly down on the water in a different direction from where it is picked up.

Tension cast

One of these is the **tension cast** which is very simple to execute but very effective and used a lot by **nymph fishers**. The cast begins when the fly has fished round and is on the dangle. The caster then faces upstream and sweeps the rod tip over in a wide arc, lifting the fly-line and repositioning it upstream in the process.

The Tension cast

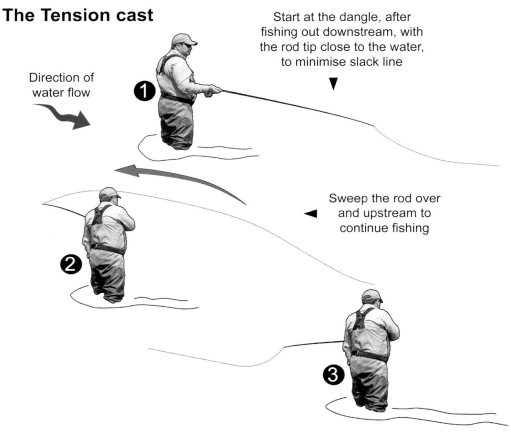

Start at the dangle, after fishing out downstream, with the rod tip close to the water, to minimise slack line

▼

Direction of water flow

❶

❷

Sweep the rod over and upstream to continue fishing

◄

❸

Star cast

It is possible to change direction by continuously false casting and moving the body round, each time, as the back cast unfurls. But this is very energy-consuming and is only really practical when your feet are standing on an even surface. This cast is known as the **star cast**.

Barnegat Bay cast

Another method is to present the fly with a short back cast. In this way the dominant casting arm is used (useful in strong winds) and the body is turned so that the cast is made over the downwind shoulder.

The Galway cast

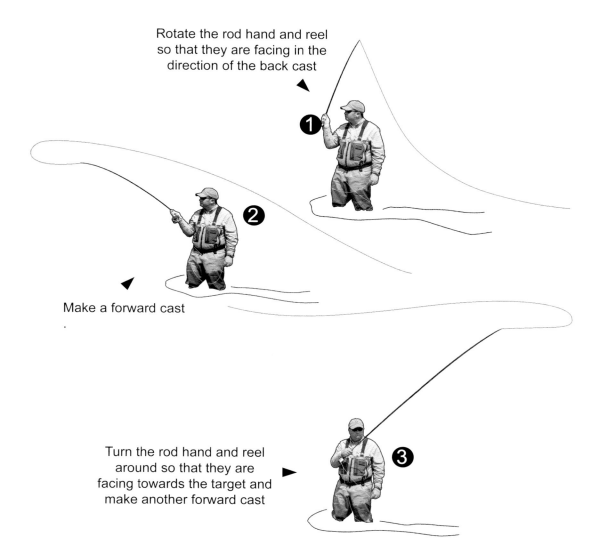

Rotate the rod hand and reel so that they are facing in the direction of the back cast

➊

➋

Make a forward cast

Turn the rod hand and reel around so that they are facing towards the target and make another forward cast

➌

The **Galway cast**, or reverse cast, involves making a forward cast, with the upper body pointing towards the target. As the fly-line is rolling out, the upper body is turned in the opposite direction, and the wrist rotated, so that the reel is facing the target and then another forward cast is made. This cast is, in effect, two forward casts.

The advantage of this cast is that it allows the caster to see where the fly is going in both directions – particularly useful when there is dense undergrowth all around. Because most casters have a stronger forward casting action, this technique allows them to throw a longer line.

Drag-free casts

Drag-free drift of the dry-fly is most important if the natural insect is to be realistically imitated and the fish induced to take it. When there are different currents in the water, which cause the fly to be pulled round by the belly of the fly-line, then the angler can employ an **aerial mend**. This places an upstream bow in the line where the current flow is fastest. By doing this, sufficient time is allowed for the fly to drift past the fish naturally, thus increasing the likelihood of a take.

Sometimes, if the current flow is slow, you may wish to put a **downstream mend** into the line so that the pull of the fly-line gives extra movement to the fly. It is a technique often used by salmon fishers with sunken lines in slow pools.

All aerial mends are applied after the stop, at the end of the power-stroke, as the rod tip follows through. A mend is created by moving the rod tip in the opposite direction to the predominant current and the distance that the rod tip is moved controls the size of the loop. The position of the loop between the angler and the fly is determined by the timing of the rod tip movement. A quick sideways and back movement immediately after the stop will induce a mend at the end of the fly-line near to the fly, whereas the same movement applied just before the line falls on the water will create a mend which is close to the angler. A sideways and back movement of the rod tip between these two positions can be used to produce a mend anywhere along the fly-line; it all depends on timing.

This concept can be taken further to create a wiggle mend which comprises a series of mends one after the other, by swinging the rod tip from side to side, whilst following the forward cast down. The sideways distance travelled by the rod tip determines the magnitude of the mends.

To create the time to make a well-formed mend it is better if a false, overhead cast is made prior to the presentation of the fly-line. By doing this it is easier to maintain the straight-line path of the line and to stop higher.

Of course this can only be applied if there is sufficient casting space for an overhead cast.

Tips for the drag-free cast

- To make a mend close to the casting position, make the mend late and low.

- To make a mend at distance, make the mend early and high.

- For small wiggle mends use the rod tip and for large wiggles move the whole rod back and forth a greater distance.

Drag-free casts

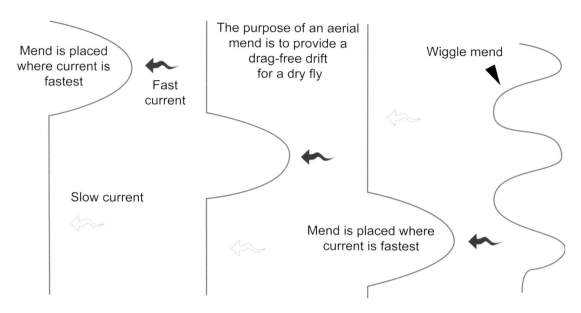

Mend is placed where current is fastest

Fast current

Slow current

The purpose of an aerial mend is to provide a drag-free drift for a dry fly

Mend is placed where current is fastest

Wiggle mend

The shape of the mend in the line will be the same as the rod tip path in the vertical plane

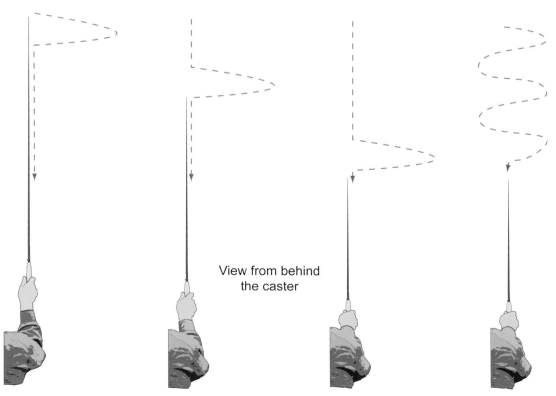

View from behind the caster

Reach mend and Curve casts

Sometimes there is insufficient headroom to make a mend – for example, when casting to a fish lying under trees on the opposite bank, or when a fish is behind a rock. For such situations there are other presentation casts which can be employed but two of the most common are the **Reach mend** and the **Curve cast**.

Reach mend

The reach mend, like all presentation casts, is used to create a drag-free drift of the dry fly. The mend is made by allowing the fly-line (held in coils on the second finger of the casting hand) to slip through the rod rings as the fly-line moves towards the target. Simultaneously, the rod is pulled back, upstream, until the rod is parallel with the water's edge and the rod tip nearly touching the water *(see page 55)*.

Fish often lie behind obstacles because these provide a comfortable and protected environment, with a slow current. They are therefore prime target areas for the flyfisher.

Curve cast

One effective method of presenting the fly to the fish is to use a **curve cast**, which bends the tip of the fly-line around the obstacle *(see page 55)*. The curve cast can also be an effective way of presenting the fly without lining the fish and spooking it.

Tips for these casts

- The difference between a **Reach mend** and a **Curve cast** is that the former is created by manipulating the rod tip *after* the power application whilst the latter is created *during* the power application.

- It is possible to give the fly-line a 90-degree change of direction by using a combination of curve and mend within the same cast.

Reach mend and Curve casts

The Curve cast

This is used for presenting the fly around an obstruction. To achieve this, the rod is given excess power, which flips the tip of the fly-line around the object (in diagram, circumventing from the right)

To circumvent from the left, cast with a sideways action, then thrust the rod forward to reduce tension in the fly-line, causing it to flop in a loop around the object

How this works:
At the end of the casting-stroke the rod is brought to an abrupt stop. Extra energy is put into the rod by reaching back and lengthening the casting-stroke. The casting arc must also be increased

The Reach mend

The reach mend can be used to the left or right side to assist with a drag-free drift of the fly

Current flow

A loop of fly-line is allowed to slip through the finger after the stop and the rod is dropped to the side, pulling more line through the rings and creating slack

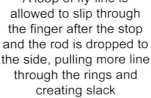

Belgian cast

A Belgian, Albert Godart, became a world champion caster in the 1930s and he used a cast with an elliptical rod tip movement. As a consequence, the various forms of elliptical casts that now exist are often referred to, collectively, as **Belgian wind casts**. However, Hans Gebertsroither, an Austrian, was probably the true originator of the oval casting technique. One of the main features of the Belgian cast is the change in rod planes between the back cast and forward cast.

The Belgian cast is particularly effective when there is a strong wind blowing from the non-casting arm side. The backcast is made low, with a loop forming below the rod tip but kept off the water (unlike the Spey cast which touches the water). The forward cast is made in the conventional overhead manner by circling up and casting near to the vertical plane. It is also possible to make this cast with a wind blowing from the casting arm side, by making the back cast with the rod almost horizontal into the wind and circling up the rod tip to make the forward cast.

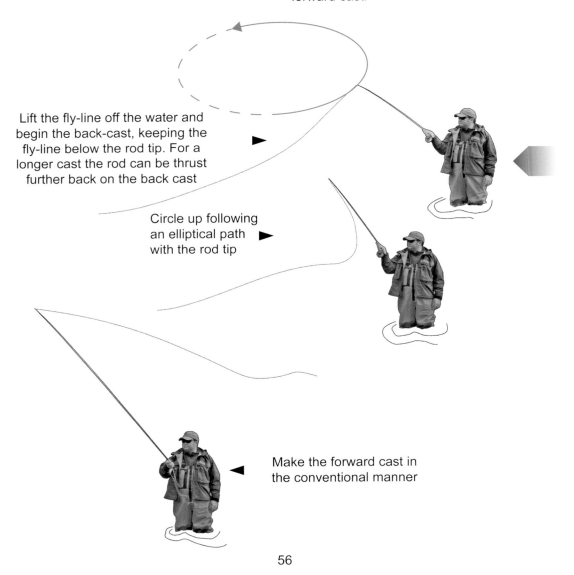

Lift the fly-line off the water and begin the back-cast, keeping the fly-line below the rod tip. For a longer cast the rod can be thrust further back on the back cast ►

Circle up following an elliptical path with the rod tip ►

◄ Make the forward cast in the conventional manner

Skagit cast

When to use it

The Skagit cast was developed by steelhead fishers in British Columbia as an efficient way of lifting heavy flies on sunken fly-lines. The technique involves the use of a sustained anchor created by using a short, heavy but bouyant, fly-line that is gripped by water tension to create good rod loading.

The perfect length of a Skagit fly-line is 3 to 3½ times the length of the rod and if a standard Skagit line is not long enough, an extension or "cheater" may be attached. Interchangeable tips with varying sink rates (ranging from floating to very fast sinking) can be joined to the end of the Skagit line with a loop-to-loop connection.

The main principles of casting a Skagit fly-line are to position the fly-line on the water, allowing it to rest for a short time, then sweeping the fly-line round and then upwards and over in one continuous movement, always using the weight of the line to keep the rod fully flexed and loaded. Therefore the Skagit cast belongs to the family of waterborne anchor casts such as the C-Spey or Circle cast, Double-Spey and Snap-T.

Ed Ward, the main protagonist of the Skagit casting movement, describes the cast by breaking it down into the following, seven, basic steps:

1) **Hang down** – feet facing the target and the rod and upper body turned, facing in the direction of the fly-line resting on the water; rod tip close to the water and the fly-line stripped back so that there is no slack between the rod tip and fly-line on the water.

2) **Pick up** – lifting the rod tip round or over to lay the fly-line on the water to position the anchor.

3) **Set** – a hesitation to allow the water tension to grip the fly-line.

4) **Sweep** – peeling the fly-line off the water, starting quite rapidly and maintaining momentum as the rod tip is swept back round, along a 35° incline, to the line-tip position (which should be resting on the casting line).

5) **45° thrust** – raising the rod tip so that the rod is canted out at 45°.

6) **Turnover** – which is the same as circling up to the key position. Note that steps 4, 5 and 6 are all one continuous movement, so that the fly-line is under constant tension.

7) **Casting stroke** – a long stroke, pushing to a stop with the top hand and pulling with the bottom hand.

Unlike conventional Spey casting, the more squiggles that are introduced into the anchor during the set, the more efficient the cast will be because this will create more resistance as the fly-line is lifted and so will develop greater rod loading. The **Perry Poke** is one refinement that can be employed to line up the fly-line ready for the forward cast and simultaneously introduce squiggles. It is frequently used in the double Spey cast immediately after the set and is achieved by inserting a relaxed dropping of the rod tip along the casting line. The **Wombat cast** is another hybrid cast which combines the Perry Poke with a Snap-T cast.

Skagit fly-line

Tips can be exchangeable, with different sink rates

Running line

Front taper

Back taper

This diagram shows the profile of a Skagit fly-line.

Wombat cast

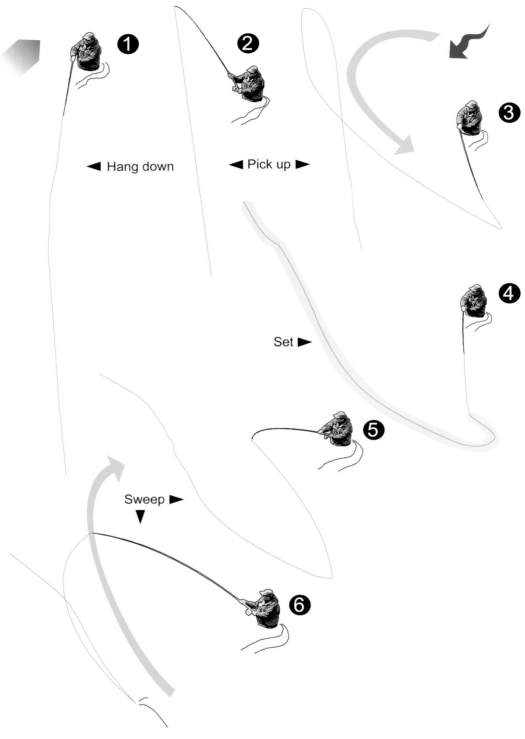

① ◄ Hang down

② ◄ Pick up ►

③

④

Set ►

⑤

Sweep ►
▼

⑥

Wombat cast *continued*

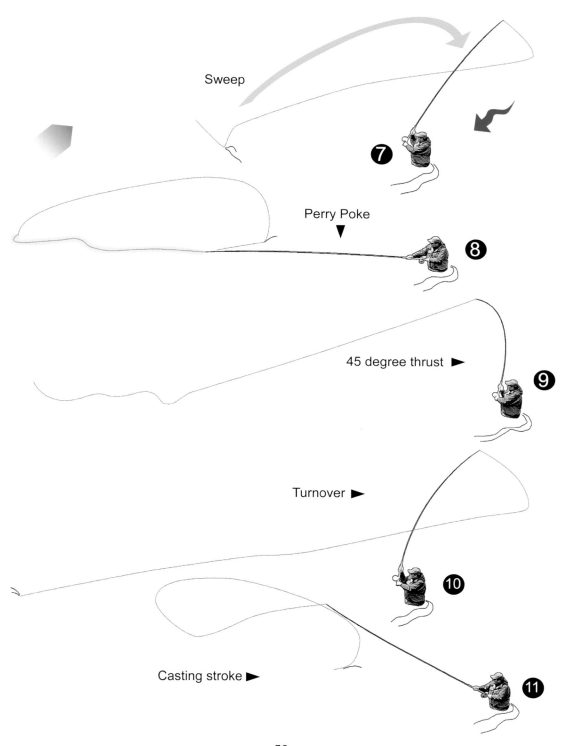

Sweep

Perry Poke

45 degree thrust ▶

Turnover ▶

Casting stroke ▶

Underhand cast

When to use it

The underhand cast was developed for use with shooting-heads and in situations where there is restricted space for making a D-loop, for example where there is dense undergrowth close to the water's edge.

Shooting-heads are 30–50 feet long and are normally used on a fast, tip-action fly rod, requiring short casting strokes. This is achieved by gripping the rod with the hands close together to obtain maximum leverage. The picture (*above*) shows that the bottom hand is used to cup the ball of the rod-butt, by wrapping the thumb and forefinger around

it, to facilitate a swivelling motion, whilst the thumb and fingers of the top hand are wrapped around the butt to create a 360 degree pivot. Very little, if any, top hand movement is used for this cast – hence the term 'underhand cast'.

The sequence of photographs (*below*) shows how the bottom hand provides most of the driving force. The elbows are kept in close to the body and there is very little evidence of circling up. Because shooting heads are short it is easy to cast them in this way. Furthermore, the heads are attached to the running line by using a loop-to-loop connection and so they can be easily interchanged and the line with the appropriate sink rate can be selected and fitted very quickly. Heads are coiled up and normally held in a wallet for ease of access.

Underhand cast

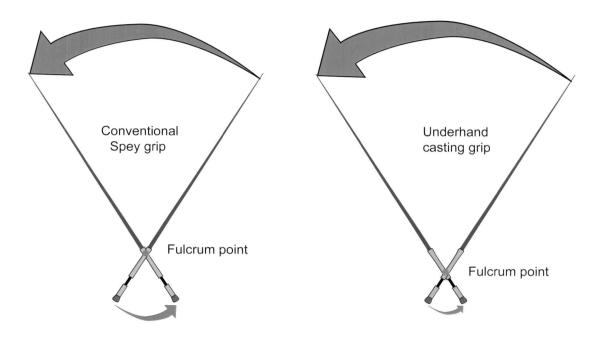

Conventional
Spey grip

Fulcrum point

Underhand
casting grip

Fulcrum point

The diagram (above) shows that by gripping the fly rod lower with the top hand, as in underhand casting, the fulcrum point gives a much greater mechanical advantage, which means that the leverage ratio is much higher. What this means is that the rod tip travels a lot faster and further for a small underhand movement. Because the shooting heads are relatively short then according to LEAPS (see page 89) the power stroke is also short, hence very high rod tip speeds and rod flex can be developed, which is one of the aims of underhand casting.

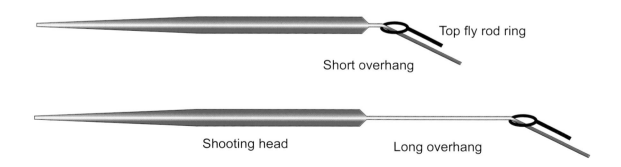

Top fly rod ring

Short overhang

Shooting head

Long overhang

A longer overhang will create a tighter forward loop.

Shooting line

One way of achieving greater casting distance is to shoot line after the casting cycle. In preparation for this, extra fly-line is pulled off the reel and stored ready for release by holding it in loops with all or one of your fingers. Holding a loop on each finger makes it easier to acquire a measured extension. At the required moment the line is released by lifting the retaining finger.

One method of doing this, with a double-handed rod, is shown in **Fig.1**. The fly-line is gathered in ever-decreasing loops, then pulled over the fly-reel to prevent the fly-line from wrapping around the reel whilst shooting. The first finger retains the loops of fly-line to be shot. Fly-line is pulled from the bottom ring of the rod using the free hand and placed over the first finger of the other hand, making a large loop initially, then forming progressively smaller loops until the fly line has been pulled in by the required amount for casting.

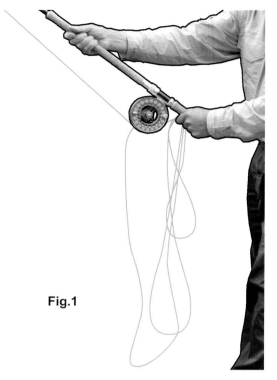

Fig.1

By storing the fly-line high up on the rod handle, the interference of the river, or bank vegetation, is minimised. The line is released by simply lifting the first finger after the stop at the end of the forward or back-cast.

Fig.2 shows one way of holding loops in a similar manner with the bottom hand but the top hand holds an additional loop, which is trapped under the first finger, and can be released whilst false casting. A greater length of line can be aerialised and a much longer cast can be made as a result.

The correct time to release the loops is after the stop in either direction.

Tips for the shooting line

- Releasing the fly-line too early will cause the rod to unload – all the energy will be lost and the cast will collapse.

- If the fly-line is released too late there will be insufficient momentum in the aerialised fly-line to pull the coiled line through the rod rings.

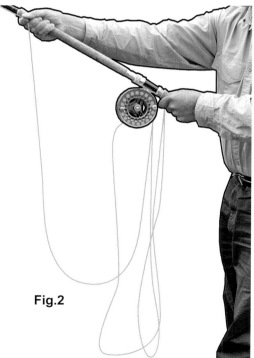

Fig.2

Line management

If the fly-line wraps around the bottom section of the rod then this is probably caused by putting too much energy into the cast.

In the case of a single-handed rod, **Fig.3** shows how the loops are held in the line hand, leaving the rod hand unhampered.

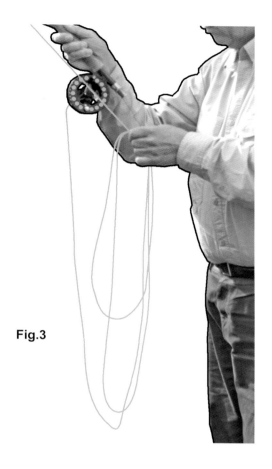

Fig.3

Retrieving

There are a number of different ways of retrieving the fly either to give it movement or to induce a take. Sometimes retrieval is not necessary at all and the fly or flies can be fished static, as is the case with buzzer fishing during hot, calm days.

Stripping or hand lining is one of the most intuitive methods of retrieving and this involves pulling in lengths of line through the rings, with short or long pauses in-between. Double pulls followed by a pause can also be used. Very fast stripping with fast-sinking lines and lures can often be productive when other methods of boat fishing fail but it is a very energetic style and can be tiring if it is employed all day.

The figure-of-eight retrieve creates a rythmic, jerking movement of the fly, similar to many aquatic life forms.

Double-handed (or Roly-poly) retrieval involves placing the rod butt under the arm and using both hands to strip back the line quickly and smoothly. This is also used with fast sinking lines and lures.

Other methods include a take-induced one by lifting the rod tip at the end of the retrieve and leaving the bob fly on the dangle. In certain conditions this can be an extremely successful way of fishing.

Fly rod characteristics

How the rod casts a line

Most flyfishers strive to cast with tight loops of fly-line, sometimes over a long distance. This is achieved by producing a fast fly-line speed, which in turn is determined by the rod tip velocity and the ability of the fly rod to store energy and to release it quickly at the end of the cast. The fly rod is required to bend continuously throughout the casting stroke and yet recover to its normal straight position as soon as possible. Both of these movements are determined by the taper of the fly rod shaft and its degree of elasticity: a sharp taper and a stiff rod will result in a quick recovery.

The stiffness is determined by the rod's diameter and the carbon density used to make it. The higher the density, the stiffer the rod, and the greater the resistance to bending and the quicker the recovery from loading. The more dense the carbon, the better the rod performs. But too much carbon makes the rod more brittle. A thicker rod will contain more carbon but can become too heavy. A compromise is required.

'Action' describes the manner in which a fly rod bends when it is loaded. Generally, fast action rods **(A)** are used for casting into high winds, or producing fast line speeds and they usually cast further than slow action rods. A fast action rod flexes in the upper third of the rod, whilst a slow action rod flexes in the upper two thirds, so consequently the latter are smoother to cast with. Tip, or fast-action rods, work well with shorter fly-lines requiring shorter casting strokes, such as shooting-heads.

Conversely, slow (or through) action fly rods **(C)** are a better choice for a more delicate presentation of the fly. Beginners find tip-to-middle action rods easier to cast with **(B)**. The amount of flexing will determine the loop shape, whilst the stiffness of the butt section dictates the pace at which the fly rod can be loaded and how quickly it unloads – the stiffer the butt section the quicker it will respond and recover. However, a stiffer fly rod will not load and store energy so easily, unless it is in the hands of an accomplished tournament caster, using a double-taper line, for instance.

Fly rod strength and length are dependent upon the type of fishing – generally larger fish, higher head-winds, bigger and heavier flies, or greater distances, would all indicate the need for a longer and stronger fly rod.

Then there are practical considerations, including something that is easily overlooked, which is ease of portability. A four-piece fly rod is easier to fit into the boot of a car or to transport on a plane, than a fly rod with three sections.

Expensive fly rods do not improve casting ability and are not necessarily the best value for money. Cheaper fly rods may not be as durable or have such a good finish or be furnished with quality fittings.

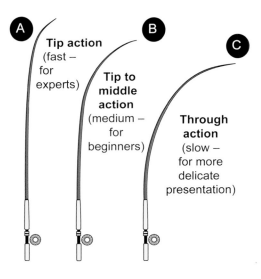

Above: Typical actions of fly rods, showing the differences in flex for each type.

For single-handed rods there is a choice of handle styles according to personal preference. A cigar-shaped handle (D) is best for a delicate presentation, whereas a full (A) or half wells grip (B and C) enable a powerful grip – good for distance casting or for using a heavier rod.

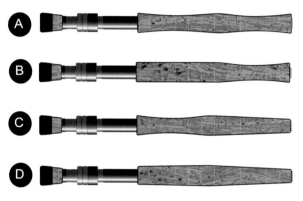

Rod butts – from top down:
Full wells, half wells, reversed half
wells and cigar-shaped rod grips.
The reel seats are up-locking.
and there is a small 'fighting butt'
extension fitted.

Reel seats can have either up- or down-locking rings but the latter is more practical for fitting the reel, particularly on the heavier rods because the reel-foot can be inserted in the bottom recess whilst the rings are locked down. There is a North American Fly-Tackle Trade Association (NAFTA) standard for the spacing of reel-foot sizes and so a large reel cannot be fitted easily on to a small fly rod.

Sometimes, on heavier rods, an extension handle is fitted below the reel seat and this is known as a fighting butt. It can be used to gain extra leverage when playing a fish. Two-handed fly rods have a longer grip and fighting butt for the same reason but they also help to reduce the need for physical strength during casting.

Cork is used for constructing the grip because this has a reduced damping effect on the flexing of the fly rod and it is not affected by water.

Rod rings

Rod rings channel and support the fly-line along the rod shaft to the rod tip. Their main purpose is to allow the maximum amount of energy transfer to the fly-line. The first rings are called stripper rings *(see page 2)* and these are used to smooth out the vibrations in the running line as it is pulled through the rings during shooting. They are fairly large rings, designed to give as little resistance as possible to the line as it passes through at speed. The second ring up from the butt is normally smaller than the first.

Snake rings are the most commonly used for the remainder of the fly rod, except for the rod tip *(see page 2)*. These have double-leg mountings, so whipping is required on both sides which stiffens up the fly rod. Single leg rings are good for when a fast response time is required. Silicone carbide (SiC) rings are the lightest, most hard-wearing and the most expensive. Titanium rings are fitted to some fly rods, which are also strong and hard-wearing and the single-leg mounting allows them to bend. At the rod tip a hay-fork ring is normally fitted *(see page 2)*.

Rings are attached to the fly rod using wraps of thread, applied under tension, by hand, or using a wrapping rig for greater precision. Two or three coatings of two-part, flexible, epoxy are then applied and allowed to dry as the rod section is slowly rotated. The ferrules can likewise be wrapped to give them additional strength.

The top ring is normally glued in position using a waterproof hot-melt adhesive and can also be wrapped to provide additional strength. On some fly rods, decorative strips are wound around the outer edges of the ring and ferrule wraps but these have no practical value and serve only to enhance the appearance of the fly rod.

Casting mechanics

The flyfisher will be aware of loop control and how a tight forward loop plays a critical role in overcoming wind resistance, transferring energy down the fly-line and providing good presentation of the fly to the fish. Sometimes, however, there may be a need to open the forward-loop such as when boat fishing with a team of flies (to avoid tangles) or when casting a particularly heavy fly.

The fly-line is simply a flexible casting weight and the rod is the means of delivering it. The bending of the rod stores potential energy – by moving the rod against a resistance. It becomes

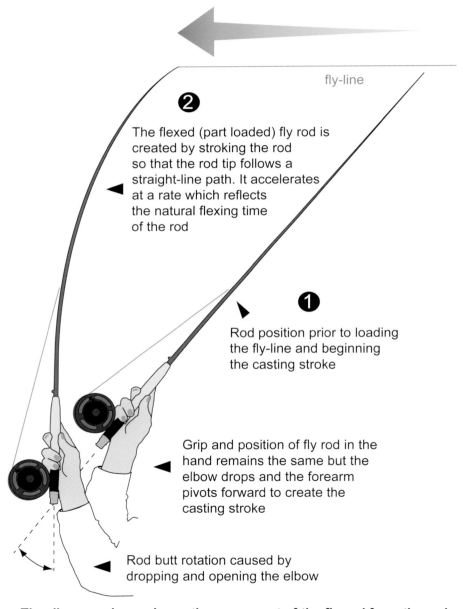

fly-line

2

The flexed (part loaded) fly rod is created by stroking the rod so that the rod tip follows a straight-line path. It accelerates at a rate which reflects the natural flexing time of the rod

1

Rod position prior to loading the fly-line and beginning the casting stroke

Grip and position of fly rod in the hand remains the same but the elbow drops and the forearm pivots forward to create the casting stroke

Rod butt rotation caused by dropping and opening the elbow

The diagram above shows the movement of the fly rod from the rod loaded position to the flexed position.

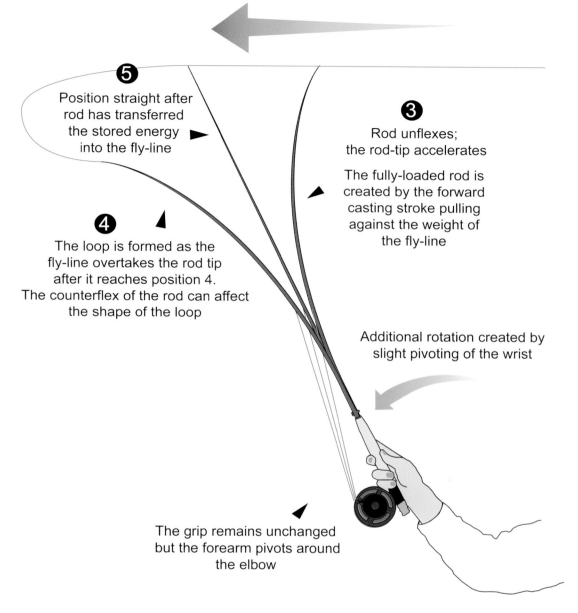

⑤
Position straight after rod has transferred the stored energy into the fly-line ▶

③
Rod unflexes; the rod-tip accelerates

The fully-loaded rod is created by the forward casting stroke pulling against the weight of the fly-line

④
The loop is formed as the fly-line overtakes the rod tip after it reaches position 4. The counterflex of the rod can affect the shape of the loop

Additional rotation created by slight pivoting of the wrist

The grip remains unchanged but the forearm pivots around the elbow

The diagram above shows the fly rod unloading during the stop, straightening out and then going into counterflex.

a 'loaded' fly rod. In aerial casts, when the fly-line is in the air, the resistance is created by the fly-line either behind or in front of the fly rod. In water-borne casts it is created by the anchor of the fly-line on the water and the weight of the fly-line against the rod.

Consider the forward-cast, with a single-handed rod and approximately 45ft of fly-line, measured from the fly-reel to the end of the tippet, where the fly is attached. The cast begins with the rod held up in the hand with the thumb (or finger depending on the grip) just in front of the eye on the side of the casting-arm. The fly-line has just unfurled behind and is just about to unfurl completely when the forward casting stroke is started. The caster then starts to move the casting hand forward with a gradual acceleration in the direction of the cast and as a consequence the fly-line is pulled in the opposite direction to where it was previously travelling and the resistance/weight of the line being pulled through the air will start to bend (load) the rod in the opposite direction of travel.

The caster increases the speed of travel with a progressive acceleration, causing the rod to load deeper and the fly-line speed to increase. This continues until the caster starts to reach the correct stroke distance and acceleration required for the length of fly-line being cast. By doing this the rod and fly-line will have stored sufficient energy to cast the fly-line, providing the energy is transferred efficiently.

Throughout the casting stroke the path of the rod tip should be held in a straight line in the vertical and horizontal planes (see page 83), not only to ensure an efficient transfer of energy but also to propel the fly-line with the correct trajectory.

As the hand holding the rod comes straight in front of the caster with the casting-hand thumb (or finger depending on grip) pointing directly up, the hand is stopped abruptly. However, in reality, because of the momentum of the fly rod, the hand does continue to move forward and so this action could be more accurately described as a controlled deceleration.

During the stop, the rod will be bent with the curve of the bend pointing in the casting direction. The grip of the casting hand is softened after this point to prevent any shock waves developing in the rod and then on into the fly-line. The curve will start to straighten out until it reaches what is known as the Rod Straight Position (RSP).

As the rod straightens, the rod tip is travelling at its fastest and when it reaches peak velocity, all of the energy that was stored during the bending of the rod, in addition to that directly imparted by the caster into the fly-line, will have been transferred to the fly-line.

After the rod straight position, the rod starts to bend in the opposite direction of the cast and the fly-line is restrained at the rod tip which causes a forward-loop to form. Further energy is fed into the forward loop by the counterflexing of the fly rod. The loop assumes the shape of a half circle of line. The section of the fly-line that continues to move is called the 'fly leg', simply because the leader and fly are attached to it, whilst the bottom section of fly-line that is attached to the rod tip is known as the 'rod leg' and this part of the line does not move.

The loop may be further widened during the stop phase of the cast by continuing to rotate or tilt the rod sloping away from the caster. This will lower the rod leg of the line as the rod tip is lowered. Another less efficient way is to cast with the rod tip following a convex path.

The rod bend then recovers and returns to the RSP but any smaller movement backwards of the rod tip is then known as rebound. Some of the energy created in the bend is lost but the majority should travel down the fly-line at the point where the loop front is formed.

A way to picture this is to imagine there is a roll of carpet, nailed down at the top of a flight of stairs and when pushed off the top it unrolls. As the line unfurls completely and the energy dissipates, the line can be presented to the water by lowering the rod in line with it, or alternatively the caster can go on to their next cast.

Fly-lines

Fly rods can be likened to whips with varying degrees of stiffness. The degree of stiffness is calculated by the fly rod manufacturer and all manufacturers design to the same stiffness scale so that, in theory, all fly-lines and fly rods are balanced and interchangeable. The scale most widely adopted is called the AFFTA (American Fly Fishing Trade Association) rating, which is given in the table below.

The AFFTA ratings are based on the weight of the front 30-foot section of the fly-line.

AFFTA Number	Line Weight			Tippet Strength (lbs)	Size of fly
	grains	grams	ounces		
1	60 ± 6	3.9	0.14	4	12 - 20
2	80 ± 6	5.2	0.18		
3	100 ± 6	6.5	0.23		
4	120 ± 6	7.8	0.27		
5	140 ± 6	9.1	0.32	6	10 -16
6	160 ± 8	10.4	0.37	6 - 8	8 - 14
7	185 ± 8	12	0.42		
8	210 ± 8	13.6	0.48	8	Leaded lures
9	240 ± 10	15.55	0.55	10	Heavy tubes
10	280 ± 10	18.15	0.64	10 -15	
11	330 ± 12	21.4	0.75	12 - 20	
12	380 ± 12	24.6	0.86		
13	450 ± 15	29.2	1.03		
14	500 ± 15	32.4	1.14		
15	550 ± 15	35.6	1.26		

The AFFTA single-handed rod rating table

Spey fly-line weights

Fly-lines for double-handed fly rods use a different rating scale and there are four categories (*see below*) which are based on head length.

AFFTA Number	Shooting head < 50ft long at 40ft		Short belly 50 - 60ft long at 55ft		Mid belly 60 - 70ft long at 65ft		Long belly Over 70ft long at 80ft	
	grains	grams	grains	grams	grains	grams	grains	grams
5	210	13.6	380	24.6	420	27.2	560	36.3
6	250	16.2	420	27.3	460	29.9	600	39.0
7	300	19.5	470	30.5	510	33.1	650	42.2
8	360	23.4	530	34.4	570	37.0	710	46.1
9	430	27.9	600	39.0	640	41.6	780	50.6
10	510	33.1	680	44.2	720	46.8	860	55.8
11	600	39.0	770	50.0	810	52.6	950	61.7
12	700	45.5	870	56.5	910	59.1	1050	68.2

The AFFTA double-handed rod rating table

There is also another rating scale for Skagit lines. These are lines that have a short, buoyant body designed to make it easy to turn over an interchangeable heavier tip, which can be helpful for fishing in restricted spaces. Skagit lines are designed for use with fast-sinking tips and heavy flies.

Skagit Heads		
AFFTA No.	grains	grams
5	400	25.9
6	450	29.16
7	550	35.64
8	600	38.88
9	650	42.12
10	750	48.60

Fly-lines

Your choice of fly-line will depend on the size of fly, fishing depth, speed of current, casting space, water temperature, prevailing wind strength and casting distance. Most casters are concerned with creating tight loops, which reduce wind resistance and give a good turnover to the fly.

Once the fly-line has been cast out, then its behaviour in the water has to be considered. For example, to avoid skating the fly along the water's surface it is common practice to attach an intermediate tip to the fly-line. Sometimes the fish can be way below the water's surface and so a sinking line is the best way of reaching them. There is a wide selection of speciality lines available for all conditions and styles of fishing. Multi-tip lines have been developed and there is a range of shooting heads which are loop-to-loop connected to a running line for a quick change-over. Thus, it is not necessary

for the modern angler to carry lots of reels or spools.

The most widely-used fly-line is probably the weight-forward floater, which gives the best combination of turnover and distance, and it is also easy to roll cast. However, many modern fishers are using shooting heads because they are versatile and can be used effectively in confined casting spaces (for instance where a high river bank, trees or undergrowth inhibit the back cast). These lines are relatively short and available in a variety of densities from floating to fast-sinking, including density combinations such as an intermediate/sinking line.

Some fishers prefer to use double taper fly-lines because they find them easier to roll cast and consider that they give a better presentation but this is a question of personal preference.

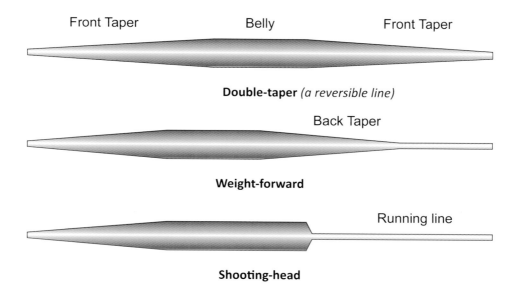

Front Taper   Belly   Front Taper

Double-taper *(a reversible line)*

Back Taper

Weight-forward

Running line

Shooting-head

Above: A selection of typical fly-line profiles

Fly-line characteristics

You can buy long head lines and short head lines

Long heads are used when there is adequate room for a back cast: they produce a longer loop, longer distance and accurate presentation with less stripping of the line and are easier to mend.

Short heads are selected when there is limited back-space. They are used with faster rod actions (shorter strokes) and are better for sink-tips, windy conditions and bulky flies. Distance is achieved by shooting line.

Head

Front Taper | Body | Back Taper | Running Line

Line shapes and thicknesses

Diameter of front section of fly-line determines the amount of energy delivered to the leader.

Larger diameter = transfers more energy
Smaller diameter = loses more energy
Front taper determines the rate at which the unrolling loop accelerates
Greater taper = faster acceleration

Small diameter **running line** is easily pulled through the rod-rings, offering some resistance to give line turnover.

The larger the diameter the less prone it is to tangling and the easier it is to strip line.

A **long taper** (above) with small line diameter enables delicate presentation. It slows the unrolling loop and is **good for roll-casting**.

The **back taper** provides a smooth transition from the body to the running line.
Long back tapers assist with mending.
The back taper can be extended to bring the head mass further forward, thereby helping to pull the running line out of the rings, and increasing energy transfer from the fly rod.

A **short taper** (above) with large line diameter is **best for bulky flies**, delivering more energy to the leader. It brings the weight of the line to the front and helps to pull running-line out through the rings.

Sink tips

Sink-tips are used for fishing in fast-flowing, deep water. They help to present the fly at the right depth.

Tips range from *very fast* to *slow-intermedate* sink rates, or combinations of two different sink rates.

A **medium/fast taper with small diameter** (above) gives accuracy and accelerates and smooths the unrolling loop.

Compound tapers (above) can be used for creating particular casting characteristics such as **extended flight**.

Other fly-line profiles

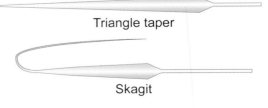

Triangle taper

Skagit

A **short taper** (above) **with large diameter** and **forward body weight** delivers more energy to the leader. Ideal for windy conditions.

Planes

As they develop their skills, flycasters will find that there is a need for references which they can use to explain basic casting techniques and to analyse and identify casting faults. One of the most widely-used of these references is the straight line, and closely related to this is the plane. A plane can be described as an infinite number of imaginary straight lines, placed side by side in one direction only, in free space (*see below*).

Horizontal and vertical planes describe an imaginary set of parallel horizontal and vertical straight lines, above and on either side of the caster. The rod tip, during the forward or back cast, follows these imaginary lines.

For a basic cast in which the fly-line is required to be aerialised in a horizontal path, the rod tip must follow a straight path in both the vertical and horizontal planes, from the beginning to the end of the casting stroke. In other words when looking from above or from the side, the rod tip must move in a straight line in the direction of the cast. When the cast is made

correctly, a tight forward loop will be formed and there will be an efficient transfer of energy from rod to fly-line.

In the horizontal plane the straight line that is automatically selected by the caster is the one which converges on the target (fish location) and starts from the position where the rod tip has finished at the end of the back cast. The straight lines in the vertical plane are stacked above and below this straight line and the one that is automatically selected is the one that also starts from the rod tip position where the back cast has finished. The straight lines in the vertical plane do not have to be horizontal, as is shown later in this section.

There are two main casting faults associated with deviation from a straight-line path of the rod tip in the vertical plane. An open loop that travels along the fly-line after it has been cast indicates that the rod tip has not followed a straight-line path in the vertical plane and that it has gone through an upward-curving or convex path.

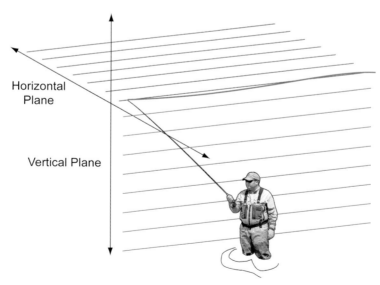

Horizontal Plane

Vertical Plane

The diagram above shows the imaginary lines in the horizontal and vertical planes. They have only been shown up to, and to the right side of, the fly-line for clarity, but they could extend on the other side of the aerialised fly-line as well.

When the line tip crosses under the belly of the fly-line and often collides with it, this is known as a **tailing loop**, and has been caused by not maintaining a straight-line path with the rod tip and causing it to pass through a downward-curving or concave path instead. The cause of this is the use of too much rod-tip speed at the beginning of the casting-stroke or stopping the rod tip too early at the end of the casting stroke.

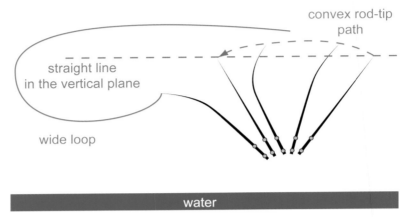

The above diagram shows how a rod-tip path which deviates from the straight line in the vertical plane by curving upwards (convex) causes an open loop.

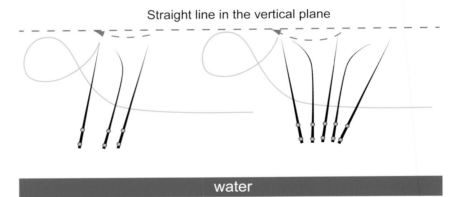

The diagram above shows two examples of how a tailing loop may result from not following a straight line path in the vertical plane. The example on the left hand side shows how stopping the casting stroke too early, causes the rod tip to rise as the fly-rod unflexes, thus creating a concave rod-tip path. A tailing loop is created in the example on the right hand side by applying power too early in the casting stroke, which causes the rod tip to decelerate early and the rod to prematurely unflex and then flex again at the end of the casting stroke.

Deviations from a straight line rod-tip path in the horizontal plane will cause the fly-line to swing, in the opposite direction to the curve traced by the rod tip during the casting stroke and this is referred to as a **tracking fault**. The straight line selected in the horizontal plane will normally run from where the rod tip starts at the beginning of the casting stroke to the point targeted by the caster. The fault is usually caused by the casting hand not following a straight line, or by excessive body rotation.

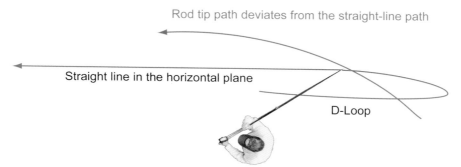

Rod tip path deviates from the straight-line path

Straight line in the horizontal plane

D-Loop

This shows the rod-tip path deviating from a straight line in the horizontal plane, causing a curved forward cast – in this instance curving to the left-hand side of the caster.

Other planes that can be used for reference are the **casting plane**, **line trajectory**, **upper body alignment** and **rod plane**.

The **casting plane** is used to describe the straight-line path that the casting hand should take through the casting stroke. This should remain straight in the horizontal plane to avoid tracking issues.

Line trajectory

The straight lines in the vertical plane need not be horizontal and usually they are at an angle to the horizon, depending upon the distance to the target. A long line requires a high, forward trajectory whereas a short line and a closer target would be cast downwards, as shown in the diagram below. This series of lines can be better described as the **line plane**. This provides a more practical way of describing the straight line path that the rod tip and fly-line travel during

a cast. It is very important that the overhead back and forward casts are both kept in the horizontal plane and in the same line-plane, which is known as the 180° rule, although this rule can be broken from time to time as in the case of the overhead-cast with a change of direction.

Upper body alignment describes the series of imaginary lines that start from the toe to head centre of the caster's body and extend out in the direction of the caster's target.

Rod plane

The rod can, of course, be held at any angle, on either side of the caster's body, limited only by the rod tip touching the ground or surface of the water. This angle, relative to the body, determines the rod-plane, which is a set of imaginary parrallel lines (see diagram on page 86).

These two planes are useful for describing the position of the fly-rod in relation to the caster's body.

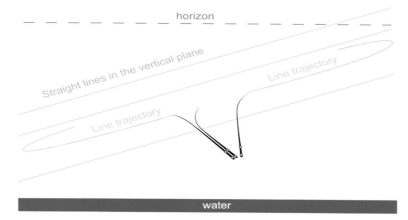

horizon

Straight lines in the vertical plane

Line trajectory

Line trajectory

water

The diagram left shows the line trajectory, which is one of the lines in the vertical plane but these are at an angle to the horizon. The slope of the line can be downwards or upwards depending on the distance to the target. It is important that the back and forward casts are in the same line trajectory and 180 degrees opposite to each other.

The diagram to the right shows the upper body alignment which should line up with the target and converge with the rod plane.

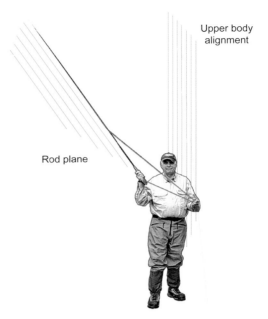

Upper body alignment

Rod plane

Side casting

A simple way for beginners to understand the basic principles of timing, loop formation and straight-line path is to cast on the side of the body. By doing this it is possible to observe both the forward and the back cast without introducing a lateral loop. Because the wrist-pivoting movement is more predominant, it is easy for the caster to focus on this and to perfect just this element of the casting action.

This exercise can be practised on grass with two cones which can be used as aiming points *(see diagram below)*. One of the objectives is to achieve nicely-formed loops which roll out

in both directions but the same set-up can be used for developing the double or single haul. The fly-line can even be laid on the ground at the end of both the forward and back casts before proceeding in the opposite direction.

Once horizontal casting has been mastered, the rod can gradually be raised to the vertical plane and then over to the horizontal plane on the other side of the body.

The horizontal cast is a useful cast in its own right and can be used to cover fish that are sheltering under overhanging trees, or for cutting into the wind.

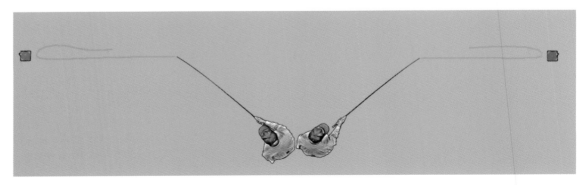

Practicing the side cast on grass, with cones

Loops

From the shape of the loop it is possible to diagnose casting faults. The fly leg and the rod leg of the loop should be parallel to each other in the vertical plane (looking from the side) and the horizontal plane (looking from above). Deviation of the rod tip from the straight-line path during the casting stroke will cause the fly- and rod-legs to be non-parallel. There is a technique that is used to analyse the loop, relate this to the rod movements, and then to the caster's movements, in order to find the cause of loop faults. The process is then reversed going from the caster to the rod and then the line, introducing corrections at each stage to correct the fault.

When the line crosses itself

One common fault in casting is the tailing loop (when the line crosses itself) and this occurs when the rod-tip is forced through a concave path (*see page 78*).

Several actions of the caster can cause this to happen:

- an abrupt acceleration at the beginning of the casting-stroke (starting too fast and not able to maintain an acceleration)

- too short a casting stroke

- or insufficient rod-arc
  (see section on LEAPS).

The rod should be continuously accelerated from slow to fast, through the casting stroke, with the correct stroke length and casting arc.

A convex (dome-shaped) rod-tip path will cause an open loop and the size of the loop is determined by the distance below the straight-line path at which the rod tip comes to rest. The main reason for open loops is too wide a casting arc.

It is also important to maintain parallel loops in the horizontal plane (looking from above) and lateral loops are a common problem, as is curving of the fly-line, to the right or left, at the end of the cast. These are often referred to as 'tracking faults' and the main causes are unnecessary shoulder movement or rotation of the body or wrist.

The caster should strive for a straight-line path throughout the stroke, unless the cast is an unconventional one such as the curve cast which introduces a mend during the casting stroke by creating a curve on purpose. In fact if the rod-tip is raised close to the straight-line path at the end of the cast, this will have the effect of tightening up the loop. However, in certain circumstances, such as high winds, or when casting heavy flies, or a team of flies, an open loop is desirable and this is achieved by bringing the rod tip down lower, after the stop.

Loops

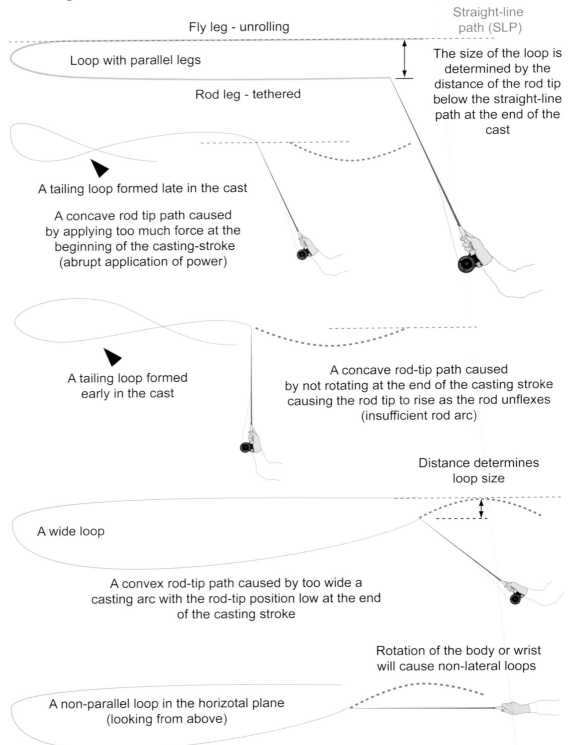

Fly leg - unrolling

Straight-line path (SLP)

Loop with parallel legs

The size of the loop is determined by the distance of the rod tip below the straight-line path at the end of the cast

Rod leg - tethered

A tailing loop formed late in the cast

A concave rod tip path caused by applying too much force at the beginning of the casting-stroke (abrupt application of power)

A tailing loop formed early in the cast

A concave rod-tip path caused by not rotating at the end of the casting stroke causing the rod tip to rise as the rod unflexes (insufficient rod arc)

Distance determines loop size

A wide loop

A convex rod-tip path caused by too wide a casting arc with the rod-tip position low at the end of the casting stroke

Rotation of the body or wrist will cause non-lateral loops

A non-parallel loop in the horizotal plane (looking from above)

LEAPS

The acronym **LEAPS** is used to remind the caster of the various changes that have to take place when a longer cast is desired and the line length changes. The letters stand for:

Line - the length of fly-line outside the rod-tip
Energy - the energy required to load the fly-rod
Arc - the casting arc
Pause - the time required for the loop to straighten
Stroke - the casting stroke

Long casts

When you a need to cast a longer line, several things must also be increased. Firstly, more energy must be stored in the fly-line to create the necessary force required to launch the heavier line. The greater weight of the line helps to load the rod during the back cast.

The energy increase is achieved by accelerating the rod over a longer distance and the casting-stroke must therefore be longer. The rod will flex more and so, to maintain the straight line path of the rod tip, the casting arc must be more pronounced. This will increase the rod-tip speed

which in turn will transfer more energy into the cast. With a longer length of line aerialised during the back cast, the pause must also be longer to allow the fly-line to unfurl fully.

Another consideration is that the line path of the cast should be sloping slightly upwards to increase the flight time and to compensate for the pull of gravity, which causes the fly-line to fall.

It is very important to remember that the opposite to all of these rules applies to a short cast.

Long cast

Short cast

The two photographic sequences above show *(top)* **the difference in body stance, stroke and arc for a long, and** *(bottom)* **short length of fly-line.**

LEAPS - Casting a longer **Line** requires a greater amount of **Energy** in the fly rod, a wider casting **Arc**, a longer **Pause** and a longer **Stroke**

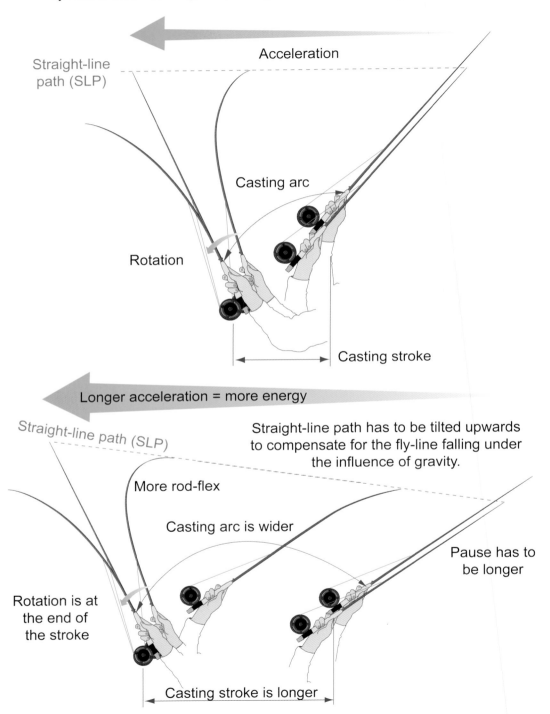

Acceleration

Straight-line path (SLP)

Casting arc

Rotation

Casting stroke

Longer acceleration = more energy

Straight-line path (SLP)

Straight-line path has to be tilted upwards to compensate for the fly-line falling under the influence of gravity.

More rod-flex

Casting arc is wider

Pause has to be longer

Rotation is at the end of the stroke

Casting stroke is longer

Glossary of casting terms

Term	Explanation
Acceleration	The rate at which an object changes its velocity.
Anchor	Length of fly-line tip or leader that is held by water tension whilst the D-loop is formed.
Casting arc	The angle moved by the rod butt between stops.
Casting cycle	All the movements of the fly rod required to complete a cast.
Casting stroke	The movement of the casting hand (top hand) from the start to the finish of a cast.
Circle up	Continuous upward rotating movement of the rod-tip during D-loop formation.
Closed stance	Foot under the casting arm (top hand) is placed forward, and body/arms are lined up with the cast, with limited body rotation, to provide greater casting accuracy.
Counterflex	Reverse movement of the fly rod after unloading.
Creep	Casting fault caused by premature movement of the fly rod in anticipation of a cast, which reduces the casting stroke length.
Displacement	Refers to how far out of place an object is.
D-loop	The shape of the loop of fly-line that is formed behind the rod-tip during the back-cast of a Spey cast.
Drag	When the fly is pulled across the water by the fly-line, unnaturally.
Drift	Deliberate movement of the fly rod, in the same direction as an unrolling fly-line to allow it to extend, which also increases casting stroke length.
Efficiency	Maximum generation of energy for the minimum input of effort.
Hinged lift	Raising a double handed fly rod with the top hand using the bottom hand as a pivot, bringing the rod-tip up high.
Horizontal plane	View of the cast looking from above.
In-swing	Moving the rod-tip in towards the bank, after the lift and prior to making a single Spey cast, helping the fly-line to peel off the water and assisting with the change of direction of the cast.
Key position	Positions of hands and rod for making a forward cast.
Kinetic energy	The energy generated in a fly rod due to its loading, which is released when the fly rod straightens.
Lateral	Sideways.
Lift	The initial raising of the fly-line, off the water, at the beginning of a cast.
Line stick	Length of fly-line held by water tension.
Loading	Creation of kinetic energy by moving the mass of the fly-line with the fly rod causing it to flex.
Loop	The U-shape of the fly-line, looking from the side, whilst the fly-line is in flight.

Maximum rod flex	Maximum bending of the fly rod, just before the stop, after it has been accelerated.
Minimum chord length	Distance between the rod-tip and rod-butt during maximum rod flex.
Narrow loop	A loop that rolls along the fly-line to the line-tip and has very little wind resistance.
Open stance	Opposite foot to the one under the casting arm (top hand) is placed forward and the body is positioned to allow an unimpeded, long casting movement.
Open loop	A loop that is very wide and so has little inertia and a high wind resistance.
Pause	A delay in a cast to allow the D-loop to form. Also a delay in an overhead cast to allow the fly-line to straighten.
Rod straight position	Fly rod at rest – not subjected to loading.
Rotation	Turning the fly rod to increase rod-tip speed.
Scalars	Quantities that are fully described by a magnitude (or numerical value) alone.
Shotgun lift	Raising a double handed fly rod with both hands to keep the rod-tip low.
Slack line	Fly-line between the rod-tip and fly that is not under tension.
Speed	Scalar quantity that refers to how fast an object is moving (the rate at which an object covers distance). It only has magnitude.
Stop	Quick deceleration of the fly rod to transfer the potential energy into the fly-line.
Straight-line path	Imaginary line that the rod-tip follows during the cast, essential for efficient transfer of energy from the fly rod to the fly-line and for creating narrow loops.
Thrust	Movement of the rod butt under power by the caster.
Translation	Movement of the fly rod butt in one direction, ignoring any rotational component.
Vectors	Quantities that are fully described by both a magnitude and a direction.
Velocity	The rate at which an object changes its position from a datum. It has magnitude and direction.
Vertical plane	View of the cast looking from the side.
V-loop	The shape that is produced by the fly-line during the back-cast of a Spey cast, when more kinetic energy is used in the cast.
Wrist break	Excessive pivoting of the wrist which prevents the fly rod from loading.
Wrist rotation	Pivoting of the wrist joint in the direction of the cast.

Index

Index *continued*